Touched by Angels

Other Christian books edited or written by Charles H. Muller

The Christian Teachings of Charles Kingsley
by Charles Muller

Diadem Books, 2011   ISBN 978-1908026033

The moral purpose of Charles Kingsley's novels is pronounced because he was a preacher, and more specifically, a teacher. He was above all a preacher of stirring didactic sermons.

Have Anything You Really Really Want: A Christian Testimony
by Charles Muller

An inspirational guide to achieving one's goals and dreams of success
Writers Club Press ISBN 0-595-091-539

The Cage and the Cross
A Christian novel by Charles Muller.
Writers Club Press. ISBN: 0-595-09806-1

A Christian novel of salvation based on an actual person, a prisoner in Pretoria Central Prison who committed suicide in 1975. The protagonist couldn't help falling in love, against his will. Those who knew him better tried to stop him, to draw him back, to tell him it was wrong, against the Law of God. But they couldn't stop him--because the affair was with God. Or was it? Perhaps the whole affair was just part of his imagination.

Rapture at Sea
A Christian novel by Carolyn & Humphrey Muller.
Writers Club Press. ISBN 0-595-13825-X

As the year 2000 approaches for many the prospect of Christ's promised return becomes more of a reality. So what if the Parousia, or the Rapture *does* take place?   What if Christ returns to Earth while some are at sea?   Would some be taken, and some left? What might happen to those passengers on a sea voyage?

Touched by Angels

Testimonies of Christian Power

Edited by

Charles H. Muller
MA (Wales) PhD (London) DEd (SA) DLitt (UOFS)

DB

DIADEM BOOKS

Published by Diadem Books

For information, please contact:

Diadem Books
16 Lethen View
Tullibody
Alloa
FK10 2GE UK

www.diadembooks.com

ISBN-10: 1908026499
ISBN-13: 9781908026491

Epigraph

And we know that all things work together for good
to them that love God, to them who are called
according to his purpose.

Romans 8:28 (KJV)

TABLE OF CONTENTS

Note from the Editor

WHEN MY MOTHER, who was a strong Christian believer, died in 1987, Reverend Raymond Brown told me 'heaven had become more precious' for me. Indeed, since then heaven has considerably increased in value, a number of the contributors in this book of testimonies having gone on to join the heavenly throng—Le Roche Furstenburg, Flo Pretorius, Professor Mokgokong, and the Reverend Raymond Brown included.

The memory of all the contributors to this little volume is precious to me. They are—or were—remarkable people whom the Lord had touched in one way or another, manifesting His divine love and miraculous power. It was my own unexpected experience of the Lord's power and presence that, in 1984, changed my life and caused me to forsake my academic career in South Africa and move to the United Kingdom where I could obey His injunction to write, to "feed His lambs" through the written word. It was also that remarkable experience of His power that made me seek out others whom the Lord had touched—at first while I was still living in South Africa. This little book is the result of that quest.

My own testimony ('Tapping into the Spirit') has been reprinted here from my longer inspirational work *Have Anything You Really Really Want: A Christian Testimony*.

I trust these inspirational stories of God's supernatural intervention in the lives of Christian believers—testimonies that present extra-biblical proof of God's divine power and love in the lives of Christian believers—will be a blessing and inspiration for many. Apart from the experiences described by believers in South Africa, there are testimonies from people in

England, Scotland, and the New World—the United States and Canada. It all goes to show that the Spirit of the Lord is moving throughout the World, and that wherever we are our hearts can be refreshed by the overwhelming and transforming love and power of our God. Angelic support and guidance can come from what many might describe as a 'supernatural' source, a divine intervention, as in the testimony of an angelic encounter retold by the Rev Louis Bosch; but Inez Randolph, from Ghana, shows that it can also come from real and tangible, everyday sources, and that we might just find our guardian angel right beside us. Angelic work, indeed, can be done by a human agent. My prayer is that the Lord will bless all who hold this book in their hands and that He will unleash his Miracle Power in their lives.

Charles Muller
Diadem Books
www.diadembooks.com

Foreword

"God moves in a mysterious way His wonders to perform."

THESE **WORDS** by William Cowper point us to a great and wonderful God, who reveals Himself to all sorts of different people, in different circumstances, and in different ways. Across the world, Christians testify to God's engagement with them—sometimes in ways that may seem strange to those brought up in different cultures or church traditions. However, as we meet Christians from around the world, and as we hear their stories, we discover how the love and grace of God can come to each one of us in a unique and special way. He never forces Himself upon us, but He always engages with us through new and refreshing experiences.

The Christian life is certainly not dull and uniform, and no one can complain that God is disinterested in our personal needs. Our God is a great God—and the stories that Christians tell of His grace and His goodness are always challenging, uplifting, and encouraging.

The exhortation and every one of the stories that follows is different, yet each points to a God of variety and colour and drama, a God who loves to reveal Himself to us in such a way that our senses are stimulated, our minds are stretched, our hearts are enlarged, and (more than anything else) our praise upraised.

May you be blessed as you read on!

Dr Adrian Varwell

Minister of Fort Augustus and Glengarry

Church of Scotland

Preface

THE BIBLE is the testimony to the power of God's love. To appreciate these testimonies one needs to see them in context and to sense the atmosphere of the occasion. Take for example John's gospel, chapter 9, and the story of the healing of the man born blind. The power of Christ's love and touch on his eyes and life strengthened him to give this testimony, "One thing I do know—I was blind, but now I see!" Yes, his testimony upset the religious establishment but brought joy to the Lord and his angels.

A testimony is worth repeating. This is borne out by the Holy Spirit recording the testimony of Paul on three occasions in the book of Acts. Paul himself on numerous occasions in his letters gives his testimony—for example, Galatians Chapter 1, vs 11-23.

In a preface of a book of this nature, it is my honour to give testimony to the creative literacy gifts of Professor Charles Muller. Charles and his wife Joanne were a tower of strength to me while I was the pastor of the Pietersburg Baptist church during the years 1983—1987. It is my joy and privilege to write the preface for someone whose desire is to finish the work the Lord has given him to do. This work is the book that is now in your hands.

In reading the range of testimonies that have brought praise and peace to the testifier, you the reader will again be exposed to the relevancy and imminence of God. We may not always relate to people's experiences, but the fruit must be an obedient and Christ-like spirit. This is what Professor Muller has seen in the lives of the people who testify in this book. Professor Muller's own testimony completes a set of testimonies to give you much encouragement in the fact that Jesus Christ is the same yesterday, today and forever (Heb.13:8). Whether we are delivered out of our trial or kept through it, Praise belongs to our God for He is our Peace.

Rev. Michael Taylor L.Th B.Th B.Th(Hons)

Organising Secretary,
Bible Society of South Africa
in Port Elizabeth

A REAL AND PRESENT HELP

Le Roche Furstenburg

LE ROCHE FURSTENBURG is a robust man in his early seventies. His pepper-grey eyebrows, his shock of grey hair, give him an immense sense of dignity. His Christian name, 'Le Roche,' suggesting a rock, is appropriate, for he certainly is a man of large and sturdy stature.

He came up to me after the service one morning at the Tzaneen Baptist Church. I had told the congregation about the way the Lord had intervened in my life. At the end I invited others to tell me of their experiences with the Lord. "I want to collect testimonies and put them in a book," I said. "This way many others can hear how the Lord is real to us today. Just like he was real to the Apostle Paul on the road to Damascus."

Le Roche put his hand on my shoulder and fixed me with his steady blue eyes. "Brother," he said, "I want to tell you about two of the most breathtaking experiences I had with the Lord."

I listened to the resonant warmth of his voice. He said: "Both experiences happened within a few days of each other. It was ten years ago." He smiled as he shook his head. "But what happened then is still as fresh as if it had happened yesterday."

I listened, and as I listened my skin tingled with goosepimples. I thrilled through and through to hear, once again, just how real the Lord is. I asked Le Roche to write out his testimony. I reproduce it here, just as he wrote it. It is just as I remember he told it. I remember his deep sense of conviction as his eyes held mine. This is a true story, told by a man who knows it to be true.—*Charles Muller.*

* * *

All my life I enjoyed excellent health. I certainly never had kidney problems. Never, that is, until ten years ago. That was when I woke up one night with the most excruciating pain in my kidneys! Pain stabbed through my back every time I tried to move. I woke Agnes, my wife. She was alarmed by my obvious agony and she called the doctor. He came as quickly as he could and did everything to ease the pain. He said I had infection in both kidneys. He gave me an injection, and more injections throughout the following days. He also prescribed tablets. But nothing helped. The pain continued for eight days and nights. It was too excruciating to stand up and I was confined to my bed. After a few days I was so weak Agnes had to help me turn from side to side.

In the meantime my brother and his family arrived, as pre-arranged, to take us to Durban. We had planned to have a holiday by the sea. But going with them, now, was out of the question. I was completely incapacitated by the pain, of course. So they left without me and my wife. It was a Saturday.

The following Sunday afternoon Agnes went to rest awhile. Left on my own, I felt impatient with my condition. I forced myself to my feet and managed to stagger around in the lounge. I was pressing both my hands on my back, trying to ease the pain. My heart was palpitating and I perspired like a race horse! I couldn't bear the pain any longer. I felt weak and I knew I was going to collapse. I turned round to face the balcony when a voice spoke behind me.

"Why don't you ask me to help you?"

My heart lurched and I stopped in my tracks. I didn't turn around but I knew it was the Lord. I lifted both my hands to heaven.

"Lord Jesus," I said, "I know it's you speaking. Please help me."

The pain ceased at once!

Yes, I was completely healed—in that very instant. (To this day I've never had any kidney trouble. PRAISE THE LORD!)

I went to Agnes and woke her.

"Come on, old girl," I said. "We're going to Durban!"

She sat up and looked at me in blank amazement. "You... you're..." She was too amazed to speak.

"Don't you see?" I said, lifting my hands again. "I'm well. The Lord has healed me!"

Well, we left for Durban, praising the Lord. We joined our family and spent a few days at the coast. It was on the way back that the second experience happened.

My brother and his family were travelling back behind us. There were three of us in my car—my wife, a young orphan girl of ten, and myself, all sitting in the front seat. We spent a few hours at Blood River where the Voortrekkers, under Charl Cilliers, fought against the Zulus. From there we travelled to Dundee, still in Natal. By the time we left Dundee it was already dark. It was a cold and gusty night and we kept the windows rolled up. I knew the road to Ladysmith very well, so I still travelled in front. The road has many inclines and declines on account of the hills and the valleys. Fast travelling is dangerous after dark.

Almost halfway to Ladysmith the road makes a sharp bend. There is a river on the left-hand side, one metre from the edge of the road. I usually take this bend at 90 kph (about 55 mph), but I slackened to 80 kph. When I reached the bend I tried to steer clear of the side of the road nearest the river.

But the steering wouldn't respond. The car went full-tilt into the river! Even as the front wheels went over the side, I called out, "Oh God, help!"

At that instant a pure white figure, my size, came through the closed window! It—or he—slid into the car and sat on my lap. He pushed my hands, which still held the sides of the steering wheel, to the bottom of the wheel. The figure then held the wheel with both hands. He drove us down the river, turning the car to the right to follow the flow of the stream.

And all the time I could see right through him! We missed huge boulders and deep holes of water. We travelled over obstacles just as if we were travelling on a tarmac road. After about forty metres he brought the car to a standstill, on dry ground. And then he left again—through the same closed window!

I just sat there, breathless and astounded. It had all happened in a moment, but I vividly recalled every detail in the sequence of events. All I could say was, "Thank you, Jesus, thank you, Jesus."

Now, after ten years, I'm still saying "Thank you Jesus!"

Agnes didn't feel any fear. She didn't realise what was happening. It was only after we got back into our flat that, as she put it, she got "the shivers and the shakes."

The following morning I took my car—a Peugeot 404— to the garage for a check-up. There was absolutely nothing the matter with it! Not the slightest damage was found.

If it were not for JESUS, to whom I give all the glory, I would not have been here to write and tell you about this miracle. The three of us came out of the car without a single scratch or bruise—to the astonishment of my brother and his family who were travelling behind us.

Again, I say, PRAISE BE TO GOD!

Le Roche Furstenburg

Tzaneen, South Africa

BLINDED TO SEE BETTER

Ray Absalom

I WAS BORN of a Jewish father and a gentile mother. With this background I was never encouraged, as a child, to attend either church or Sunday school. And so I grew up without knowing the Lord. The only time we went to church was either to a wedding or to a funeral. I did become a Christian, however. At the age of nineteen I was invited to attend a campaign at our local church, and it was then that I came to know the Lord as my Saviour.

But having had very little experience of church or the Bible, I knew very little about the word Faith. I had read about faith, of course. But I had no practical experience of what it meant to trust in the Lord. Then, just a few years ago, I learnt a tremendous lesson. I believe it was a lesson the Lord used to teach me about faith.

After working in the garden one Saturday, I woke up on Sunday morning with pain in my right eye. I went to church with my wife Margaret, but throughout the service my eye felt very uncomfortable. In fact, I could barely listen to the Pastor because of the pain. By the evening it was a real physical pain inside the eye.

On Monday morning I went to our doctor. He started treatment and I went to work.

On Tuesday I was telling some of my fellow workmen about the pain. One of the men, Fred, looked at me with grave concern.

"Ray," he said, "don't take any chances when it comes to eyes."

"I won't, Fred." By now I felt quite depressed. "I've been to the doctor. What else can I do?"

"You can go and see a friend of mine." His lips twisted into a smile. "Well, not a friend, exactly. He's a friend of a friend. But he's done some remarkable healings. He healed this other chap…"

"It's the Lord that heals," I said.

"Oh, sure." His smile broadened. "He prays often for folk, and they're healed."

Was this what I was looking for? Was this a message from the Lord? New hope filled my heart and the next day Fred and I went to see Ambrose Wright who was so widely known for his healing powers.

Mr Wright was a tall and wiry man with penetrating eyes. We shook hands and I felt strange in his presence. He seemed to be looking through me and his smile barely included his eyes. I felt reassured, however, when we sat around a table and Mr Wright asked that we bow our heads in prayer.

His voice was deep and resonant and I felt oddly uncomfortable. Perhaps that's why I was naughty! You see, I cheated, because I peeked through my fingers. My heart lurched when I saw he was holding a pendulum that was swinging in a circular motion. The pendulum was in his right hand and his left hand was poised over hundreds of little bottles—bottles that seemed to be filled with tablets.

Only a few minutes passed before he lifted his head and transfixed me with those strange eyes. My fingers fell from my face. Had he seen me peeking?

His words were spoken sternly, like an accusation: "I feel nothing has been accomplished."

"Oh?"

He shook his head. "I suggest you come back another time." He smiled, but his eyes seemed to glare at me.

It wasn't just the man's manner that made me feel uneasy. You see, I knew why nothing had been accomplished. The minute I saw the pendulum I recalled a book I had read by Kurt Koch, about pendulum swinging. It was an occult practice. While he had been praying I had called upon the Lord, pleading his blood upon me. I certainly didn't want to become involved in any pendulum swinging!

Obviously, I didn't go back. I returned to the doctor, because the pain was becoming worse, moment by moment. And so the treatment continued. I began to lose vision in my right eye and after ten days could barely see with it. The next time I visited the doctor he turned pale when I told him my right eye had gone blind. He dived for the phone and spoke to a specialist in Johannesburg.

The specialist turned out to be a thick set man with Jewish features. After a thorough examination of the eye he looked very grave.

"I'll have to remove the eye, I'm afraid."

He spoke softly but his words froze my heart. "Surely not," I whispered. "Can't you save it?"

He shook his head. "The infection has gone too far. If the eye isn't removed, it will go to your brain."

I felt dazed. But I heard myself saying, "Look, you do your part. God will do the rest."

Had I said that? In any case, my reply obviously impressed him. He put his hand on my arm. "I don't know about that," he said. "But I have a friend who might be able to help you."

He phoned the Dean of Ophthalmology at the Witwatersrand University. I don't think it was more than half an hour before I was in this man's hands. He looked like a professor with his white hair and black eyebrows. In fact, everyone called him 'Professor.' His blue eyes were kind and understanding. "I think we can stop the infection," he said. "My treatment will be a course of injections. All we do is inject an anti-biotic into the eyeball."

7

That sounded a lot better than removing the eye!

But I wasn't prepared for the pain. When the needle went into my eye, it was the most terrific pain I had ever felt!

The next day the Professor returned to the hospital to say I would have to receive an injection every second day. There would be nine injections in all. The prospect of living through that immense pain—eight more times!—was appalling.

The second injection was worse because I knew what to expect. The pain was so severe that my body shook. I passed out. The same thing happened after the third injection.

I couldn't take any more.

When Margaret came to see me during the visiting hour, I took her hand and spoke earnestly. "Please," I said, "I want you to bring me my gun."

"What!" Her eyes widened.

"I… I'd rather be with the Lord, Margaret. I mean it. I'd rather be with the Lord than suffer pain like this."

"Ray…" She was very perturbed. "I can't…"

"Please, Margaret," I pleaded.

Her piquant face, normally gentle and patient, was full of alarm. She stood up, fighting back the tears. "Ray…," she said, and then she ran out of the room.

She ran off to see our Pastor and shared her experience with him.

The next day John, our Pastor, came to see me. He was a close friend and sat down beside my bed. Even the vision in my good eye was blurred, now, but I was aware of John's sharp blue eyes as they bent close to mine.

"Ray," he said, "I'm going to pray for you." He spoke urgently. "I'll return tomorrow morning before your next injection."

The next morning came and he was there.

"Ray, I've been communicating with the Lord." He laid his hand on my shoulder and I looked dimly into his eyes. "I've spent many hours in prayer. I've asked the Lord to give me a word for you."

He turned to Psalm 103 and read these words to me:

> *Praise the Lord, O my soul;*
> *all my inmost being, praise his holy name.*
> *Praise the Lord, O my soul,*
> *and forget not all his benefits.*
> *He forgives all my sins*
> *and heals all my diseases;*
> *he redeems my life from the pit*
> *and crowns me with love and compassion.*
> *He satisfies my desires with good things*
> *so that my youth is renewed like the eagle's.*

He looked up and put his hand once again on my shoulder. "Ray, I believe, somehow, that the Lord is going to heal you. I don't know how. Only he knows how. But I believe he is going to."

I smiled through my misery. "I know he can."

He nodded. "But I want you to do something, Ray. I want you to do something in faith, trusting that Christ can do miracles, even today."

"Do something?"

His hand tightened on my shoulder. "Before the doctor administers the injection, Ray, I want you to stretch your hand out. Then invite the Lord to hold that hand. Ask him to take you through the experience."

I hesitated. "I... I don't know about that. I've never experienced anything like this before."

He leant forward. "That's exactly why you must do this, Ray. Ask the Lord to hold your hand."

When he left the room I thought about what he had said. Many thoughts crowded my mind. What would happen if the Lord didn't touch me? What if he didn't help me through this?"

My heart quickened as I recognised the footsteps in the corridor. By now I could barely see and I had learnt to know the footsteps of each doctor and each nurse. These were the footsteps that heralded the next injection. I lived in a world of growing darkness and fear.

The Professor entered the room with a sister. I breathed deeply to steady my galloping heart.

"Professor," I said. "Would you wait just one minute? I… I just want to talk to my Saviour, the Lord Jesus Christ." I felt it was important to pronounce his name.

"Of course." The Professor's voice was understanding.

And I stretched out my hand. I said, "Lord, by faith I trust that you will hold my hand. Please take me through this experience."

I turned to the dim outline of the doctor. "I'm ready."

The sister held my head in both her hands and the Professor's syringe once again pierced my eye.

There was absolutely no pain.

It was incredible! Each time I stretched out my hand and asked the Lord Jesus to take my hand. Each time, right up until the ninth injection, there was no pain whatsoever.

And yet the first three injections were like literal hell on earth. In fact, the nurses often commented, after the first three injections, "My, but you've gone grey overnight." It was true. I had turned grey because of the unbearable pain of the first three injections.

After two months I was discharged from hospital. Altogether, I was off work for four and a half months. Because of the tremendous number of tablets I had to take, I was still very weak. Nevertheless, after I felt my strength increase, I thought, one day, of the pendulum swinger. "I must go and see him," I thought. Somehow I wanted to tell him of my experience, of how the Lord took me through the injections.

And so, after I returned to work, I made an appointment to see Mr Wright. When he opened his front door I knew at once he had changed, somehow. His eyes were still penetrating, but there was a twinkle that softened the effect.

"I know why you've come." His voice was deep and melodious.

"Why?"

"You've come to tell me about the Lord Jesus Christ."

I was taken aback. "How did you know?"

He smiled. He invited me in, and then he told me about his experience.

His wife had contracted cancer of the breast. Through his pendulum swinging, he had tried to heal her, and had failed. Then he had made a covenant with the Lord. If the Lord healed his wife, he would destroy all his books—his whole library on the occult.

He had taken his wife to a Christian faith healer in Pretoria. And his wife was healed. True to his promise, Mr Wright took all his books which were valued at a few thousand rand, and he burnt them all in his back yard.

Somehow, I wanted confirmation about this man's conversion. I suppose the Lord knew my desire, for it wasn't long afterwards that I saw the man, again, in the commuter train I used regularly to travel from Germiston to Johannesburg. I saw his tall figure, stooping over the seated passengers, handing them Christian leaflets. And every day he would be there, making his way down the corridor of the train, stopping and talking to folk, giving out leaflets, and testifying to the commuters about Jesus Christ. This certainly gave me the confirmation I sought!

He had learnt a lesson about faith, like me. He had witnessed a miracle in the healing of his wife. And I had learnt to trust the Lord, not only for miraculous things, but as a real and ready Presence in the trials of life. I'm still blind in my right eye, but it's nevertheless through grace that the Lord gives me the strength to live each day by day.

Being blind in one eye is certainly a handicap. But I daily praise the Lord and thank him that he is a gracious Lord, and that he does work in small and in miraculous ways.

I know that what happened to me was miraculous. You see, what makes the experience so wonderful was that, each time I stretched out my hand before the injection, I felt it firmly clasped!

Ray Absalom
New Zealand

MY NEW NIPPLE[1]

Carolyn Joanne Muller

TODAY IS THE DAY I get my new nipple. It's a big day for me—a sort of landmark; the end of a journey, yet a day I'd been putting off; I'm very squeamish.

Here I lie on the operating table, trussed up like a Christmas turkey, not in foil, but in stuff that feels like tough kitchen roll. My life does seem to involve rather odd things but I suspect this is probably one of the oddest; unusual, if you know what I mean.

I am totally compos mentis, no anesthetic, no pain relief, no numbing injection, just raw me; my right breast is the only bit of me sticking out, except my head of course and the top part of that is covered in a silly white baggy theatre hat, so really, only my face is showing. Is this a face of agony? No, actually, it's looking remarkably calm. The gentle voice of a trainee nurse behind me is remarking that she can't work out how they are going to make a nipple out of what looks like plain skin. The surgeon, obviously used to being complimented, tells her to watch and be amazed. I think I'll not watch thanks but I am prepared to be amazed. I turn my head to the left as a registrar sits next to him looking businesslike. I hear instruments clattering. I feel my body tensing as I wait for the words, "Pass me the scalpel." I was told I shouldn't feel anything since the area is numb! I force my body to relax. A vague pulling feeling

---

[1] Reprinted from *Woman Alive*, April 2008 issue.

on my breast. This is okay. I can do this. The surgeon told me that this small operation is minuscule compared with what I have been through so far. Okay for him! I relax.

My mind drifts back to eighteen months ago. I'd had a small lump removed from my right breast. The operation only took about an hour and was a piece of cake. However, the tests on the lump showed a pre-cancerous condition and two weeks later I was told I would have to have a mastectomy. I can't describe the horror of that moment. I was numb with shock, blackness enveloped me. I couldn't believe it. Not *me*. This couldn't be happening to me. I fought back the terror engulfing my senses and tried to concentrate on what the surgeon was saying. "You could have a reconstruction." I'd never heard of that. Very basically all breast flesh is removed from the breast and replaced with some muscle taken from my back together with a silicone implant to build up the breast. Okay. That sounds like an option. I still felt nauseous.

I was shown photos of breasts that had been reconstructed. I saw photos of breastless chests, breasts with only the muscle and no gel pack and breasts that had the muscle plus gel pack. The nipples were missing in all the photos since nipples have breast tissue and ducts which might contain cancer cells so that looked a bit odd. The photos of the healthy breasts had the nipple shaded out – apparently they aren't allowed to show nipples at all! (What is it with nipples? You'd think they were the only part of the breast!)

I went home to lick my wounds. After two days of feeling like hell I got on my knees. Why I went two days without speaking to God I don't know. I fully recommend you do this at the *first* sign of a breakdown, not two days after! The Lord wrapped me up in a warm blanket called Grace. I became calm and stoic and found myself comforting those who found out and wanted to commiserate. The only time I cried was when people cried for me and I was feeling sorry for them! I had to remain strong for everyone else! Love oozed out of the woodwork and I hadn't realised how much I was loved till this time. I felt almost like a hypocrite—the Lord had really taken away all fear. People thought I was being brave—I was not. It was God's Grace that covered me. Corrie ten Boom gave a good example of what was happening to me. She said that if her father took her to the station he did not give her the money for the train journey *until* it was time to get on the train, *not before*, but at the time. I can testify that God gave me the Grace at the moment I needed it—it wasn't a lot of use a month before. God gives you the strength when you need it. Therefore we should worry for nothing. How often can I say to myself 'oh ye of little faith' since I find myself worrying needlessly about things. For goodness sake woman, take it to the Lord in prayer.

The surgeon was asking for a number 5 needle. Oh boy. I can feel myself getting hot. This is not good. Lord help me relax.

Someone said, "Oops!" The voice of the surgeon cut in quickly, "It's okay Carolyn, you only need worry if *I* say 'oops'!"

I'm out of here! My mind drifted. Sixteen months ago I was being drawn on by the surgeon. It looked like I was being measured for a new suit, except the pen marks were all over my breasts and back. I was still feeling calm despite the fact I had a seven-hour operation ahead of me next day. That had been on my mind a lot that first weekend after the awful news. The operation was actually eight hours but then I was asleep so knew nothing. My daughter and friends had been praying that I would feel no pain and it worked a treat. Bit uncomfortable but nothing horrendous. My breast felt heavy for some weeks, liquid collected in my back and I had to have it drained about once a week for a while. I didn't continue my exercises long enough and had to have extra physiotherapy but I am fine now. Because the cancer was caught in time it had not spread and I did not need chemo or radiation. This was a blessing.

"Would you like to look at your new nipple?" Mmm, okay. I can do that. I turned my head to the right. I was actually quite shocked since there in front of me, standing up like a mountain, was my new nipple. An hour before there had been a nipple-less breast; just a round of plain flat skin. I had got used to seeing the nothingness of it, now it was very proudly erect. It looked just like a nipple, the right colour and shape—except with bits of dark thread protruding sharply out of it. Amazing. Bigger than my other nipple but the surgeon says that will go down and look normal in a few weeks. I think the trainee nurse was as flabbergasted as I and thanked me profusely for letting her stay and watch—I wish I'd watched now!

I'd walked into the operating theatre—I don't suppose many patients do that—and now I'm walking out again. The end of the road. What a brave girl! I will have to have the stitches out in two weeks and in a few months they will tattoo the areola but that doesn't worry me.

This is one for the book, yet another new experience I tell myself, one I certainly didn't go through alone.

Postscript:

I shouldn't make light of this subject and in retrospect it didn't seem too bad but I will say that I am a total wimp—I passed out twice during the biopsy—a nurse had to hold my feet and legs in the air while they finished, but hey, I'm still here so there is a bright side.

You'd be surprised how many women come up to you, take you slightly aside and tell you, 'I had a mastectomy a few years ago.' You are not alone. It's very important to tell a friend/sister/mother/anyone, since you need backup.

My lump was found in a routine breast scan. What if I had not gone? It takes about 15 minutes, is not sore but a tat uncomfortable—don't be selfish; for the sake of your children, your husband, your sisters and brothers, your parents. Check your breasts; go for that scan. I'm told that most lumps are nothing. I was caught in time and look at me—I'm now as fit as a dog.

Two sites I found most useful after the operation:

> www.breastcancer.org(USA) and
> www.breastcancercare.org.uk

The latter has a helpful forum where you can ask questions from other cancer sufferers, especially those who are further on than you and give you encouragement. It also has pots of helpful information.

Carolyn Joanne Muller
Stirling, Scotland

JONATHAN

Wynne Muller

> Peace I bequeath to you,
> my own peace I give you,
> a peace the world cannot give,
> this is my gift to you.
> *John 14:27 (Jerusalem Bible)*

THE BIBLE tells us we will not be tempted or tested beyond the point we can bear. If we are close to God, he will always prepare us and strengthen us for the trials and temptations of life, or provide a way of escape (1 Cor. 10:13).

This is confirmed by the experience of Wynne Muller some three years before her young son died from leukaemia. There is no doubt the presence of the Lord came to her while she was asleep one night. In a vivid and dramatic dream, she was charged with the energy and peace that comes from God. The dream was so vivid, the message so clear, that it was obviously more than a dream. It's the way God at times chooses to speak to his people, as he did to Joseph before Jesus was born.

A vision is so much more than a dream. It speaks to us through all our senses—through the eyes, the ears, and, above all, through the heart. It's a form of spiritual communication, and indeed, it's one's spirit that testifies to the truth of the experience.

Wynne and John Muller were able to live through the experience of losing their son because of the strength they received. The supernatural, or extra-terrestrial source of this strength was clear for Wynne, because of the all-embracing spiritual experience of her dream. It's extra-biblical proof, again, of God's mighty and loving existence.

But before we listen to Wynne's own account of the story, let's hear something about Jonathan who was taken away from her. Knowing something of him will help us share something of the agony and the miracle of her experience. Perhaps the best account of Jonathan and his short life is that which appeared just after he died, in the *Vryheid Gazette* of Friday 23rd June, 1978:

> On the 29th December 1967, John and Wynne Muller were blessed by the birth of a little boy—Jonathan. To them he was a gift from God. In fact so strongly did they feel about this that like Hannah of old, they were certain that he would one day enter the Ministry and in this way they would give him back to God.
>
> And so Jonathan grew up—a happy little boy, full of fun and mischief, ready to romp and play all the time, giving and receiving love wherever he went.
>
> When he was just seven years old, he grew ill and it was found to be that most dreadful disease—leukaemia. For almost three and a half years Jonathan fought against this disease most gallantly. He never complained no matter how severe the treatment, for Jonathan loved life and wanted so much to overcome his illness and be really well again. Even at the last, when he was suffering very much and was in hospital, Jonathan was still planning a holiday in Durban.

He was always a courteous and polite little boy—the perfect gentleman. He had a smile for everyone, and always remembered to thank people, for every small thing they did for him. When he needed attention at night, he would apologise for causing a disturbance and even when he was dying and wanted water, he remembered to say please.

Jonathan was also an extremely clever little boy, who wanted to learn and find out about everything he came into contact with. This thirst for knowledge made him read extensively. He loved playing chess and would challenge most people to a game.

He was wise beyond his years, for his greatest wisdom lay in his love for God. Jonathan knew and loved Jesus and often testified to this. His faith was very great and because of this he was not afraid to die. In fact, he said as much, just before he was called home on the 15th June 1978.

* * *

Now, here is Wynne Muller's testimony:

During the first year of Jonathan's illness I had a dream which, when I awoke, I knew was a message from God.

This message was so clear and real to me that I knew he was close, and would always be close to support and strengthen us with his wonderful love. I knew, deep down, that there was nothing that could happen to us. I knew that if we only rested in him, we would know only peace.

In my dream we were having tea with our Minister and his wife in the lounge. Suddenly a terrible storm blew up. The house was buffeted by the wind. Everything became dark. The wind howled and the rain poured down.

I knew my little blond boy was in his room at the end of the passage. I made my way to the room, holding the walls to steady myself. He was lying on his bed curled up and facing the wall. I lay next to him with my arm around him, as I so often did.

Quite suddenly he wasn't there. As I realised this, I realised, too, that the storm had passed.

All was calm and light and I knew Jonathan had left me for ever.

I was overcome with grief. I cried bitterly. I couldn't bear the pain. I started to say "Our Father," but much too quickly, as I always did. After the first few words I heard a man's voice saying the prayer with me—but so beautifully, calmly and slowly. I slowed my voice and we went through the prayer together. By the time I said, "For Yours is the Kingdom, the Power and the Glory, forever and ever," I knew what those words meant. A wonderful sense of peace and love surrounded me.

I shared this dream with our Minister and my dear family. The memory of it buoyed me up through all those hopeless attempts to cure Jonathan. He was flown to Cape Town to the Leukaemia specialist there, but after so many relapses and treatments little could be done for him. Eventually we were told he had about two weeks to live and we brought him home to die.

Four days before he died I heard of the death of one of Jonathan's little friends. When I told him, he said, "Don't be sad, mom. He's lucky. He's with the Lord." He looked at me and there was peace in his blue eyes. "You know, I was always afraid of leaving you and dad. I'm not, now. I'm not afraid to die."

He spoke quite openly about his leaving us.

The doctors told us to expect a haemorrhage just before the end. We knew how this would frighten Jonathan. But our Minister reminded him of his love for Jesus. "You know and love Jesus, don't you, Jon? You told your mom you weren't afraid to die." And Jonathan replied with a nod. He was dying and too weak to talk. Then, as we were saying "The Lord is my Shepherd," he opened his eyes with a look of beautiful calm. He looked up at the ceiling and right across the room before closing his eyes. He might have been asleep.

There was such peace in that room. God had kept his promise. He was with us all. There was no haemorrhage, excessive pain or fear. There was only love, peace, and—above all—His strength.

Wynne Muller
Vryheid, South Africa

* * *

Finally, here is a poem Wynne wrote about Jonathan two years before his death. It expresses something of the peace and assurance she received from God—a quality of strength which has kept her from becoming bitter or remorseful. Her courage and cheerfulness, like Jonathan's, are evidence of a power of love that transcends human understanding.

Jonathan

Golden hair and shining eyes
Happy laughter, enchanting ways.
A little late lamb—a golden boy
Who brought laughter and so much joy.
Life is a mosaic, so they say.
Were you given—to be taken away?
Are you an 'Isaac' to test our faith
For us to return you at any date?
When will it end—these endless tests, the pain?
When will you be really well again,
you ask.—Oh! if only you knew
How many have turned to God through you.
Your courage and faith have shown
How privileged we are from God to loan
And keep you here, on Earth, till He
In His wisdom, should want you for eternity.

Wynne Muller

THE ROAD TO DAMASCUS

Raymond Brown

THE REVEREND RAYMOND BROWN, a Southern Baptist from International Crusades, came over from Texas to work with the Pietersburg Baptist Church, South Africa, in evangelistic outreach. I drove three-hundred miles to a Johannesburg hotel to pick him up at the beginning of the week-long crusade. The hotel dining-room was crowded with some sixty American evangelists who were about to disperse to various cities for the nation-wide crusade in South Africa. The atmosphere was charged with American accents praising the Lord, and the power was almost tangible.

Before long a stocky, well-built man in his mid-sixties stood before me. He was soft-spoken and his hand grasped mine. I found myself looking into grey eyes made stern by the beetling eyebrows and firm chin. That was my first impression of him—an austere and serious man. But I soon realised that his apparent austerity was shot through with love and good humour. It was that capital mixture of austerity, love and humour that held people spell-bound as they listened to him during that week. On one occasion, in my living room, nine black students from my university sat around him, listening to the Gospel. After an hour five of them surrendered their lives to the Lord, publicly accepting Jesus as their Saviour.

It was a week of rich spiritual blessings in Pietersburg, and this endearing Texan, who had been a farmer, soldier, carpenter, and finally a preacher, led many lost souls to the Lord. By the time he left us, he had found a permanent place in many hearts.

Raymond is an austere figure. Yet, when he recalled his personal encounters with the Lord, his voice trembled. And every time he recalled the moment that he first met Jesus, face to face, he would nearly break down. But every time he relived the moment, he proclaimed his joy loudly through his tears.

The story that follows is a record of his testimony. It was the way he told it in my late parents' home, where I recorded his words on tape.—*Charles Muller.*

* * *

"Well, I was born in the home of Christian parents in 1920, and was taken to church by my parents before I can even remember. I was taught the Word of God in the Sunday School, and I heard the preaching in church."

Raymond eyed his listeners as he settled back in his chair. Then his eyes grew distant with memory.

"When I was ten years of age we had a revival meeting in our church there in our home community. At the end of the sermon on the first night, when the invitation was given to come forward, a boy and his sister whom I had gone to church with since school went up to be received by the Pastor.

"'Well now,' I thought, 'I could do that too'—and so I did. I answered the questions the Pastor asked me, and I was baptised that summer.

"Of course, nothing happened in here." He placed a large hand over his heart. "I'd been taught about Jesus in the Bible." He shook his head. "I cannot remember a time when I did not believe in God, in the Bible, and in Jesus. I knew they were real." He frowned thoughtfully. "But to get all salvation exactly together... well, I didn't have it at the time."

He paused, then picked up the thread of his story. We listened to the soft Southern accent laced with sadness. Occasionally, it was punctuated by a chuckle of good humour.

"Previous to this, our Pastor was preaching and he said, 'Everybody that's a Christian in here, hold up your hand.' Now this will show you just what I knew about being a Christian at the time. There in rural Texas where I lived we had Methodists, Baptists, and Presbyterian denominations. So when he said, 'Everybody that's a Christian,' I thought he meant everybody that's a member of a Christian church. And this sister of mine, that was about seven years older than me, raised her hand. Well, my mother and father did too. It seemed strange to me and this question came into my mind: 'Why does the Pastor ask people to raise their hands when he knows they're members of that Baptist Church?'

"The next day at home I asked my sister: 'How come you held up your hand last night when Brother Carter asked the Christians to raise their hands?'

"'Because I'm Christian,' she said.

"'No,' I said, 'you're not. You're a Baptist.'

"'No, that's not what it meant,' she said.

"'Then you are a Christian?'

"'Yes.'

"'Well,' I insisted, 'how do you know you are?'

"I said it that way because I wanted to tell how she knew. But she just looked at me for a moment, then turned and walked away without ever saying a word.

"Anyway, at that time my parents were farming. My mamma had a grove of Conifer trees where they watered the stock. There was a well there, where we pumped water into a trough. Well, I was playing around that trough of water one afternoon, and just out of the clear blue here comes the thought: 'You'll be preaching one day and you'll be using water.'

"Well, I didn't particularly like that thought! I wasn't interested in preaching.

"So I went on all the way through High School to my senior years.

"We were farming with a tractor when I was still in High School. One Saturday in 1939, when the war was already taking place in Europe, my daddy had some ploughing for me to do, and I went out to the barn to get the tractor. I was gassing and oiling the tractor, getting ready to go, when this thought came to my mind: 'You're going to be in the United States Army one day, and you're going to be out in the battlefield and able to tell the people about the Lord Jesus.'

"Well, I still wasn't interested in that, so I dismissed it again.

"But, as you know, Pearl Harbour came on December the 7th, 1941, and I was twenty-one years old on the 20th day of December, 1941—just thirteen days after Pearl Harbour."

Raymond smiled as he thought of his early ambitions. "All my teenage years I had lived with this one ambition— that when I got grown, I would be my own boss." He shook his head. "Well, when I got to be twenty-one, I was everything but my own boss, because I got that telegram which said: 'Greetings. Your friends and neighbours have selected you to represent your country in its armed forces.'

"So I went into the armed service in the summer of 1942." He paused and his voice saddened. "I'm sorry to say it, but I'd already been living in sin. And in the army, with no moral restrictions, and no mamma or daddy, I went to the depths of sin." He paused again. "I'm not going to describe it in detail. All I'm going to tell you is that there's no sin committed today that I didn't commit. Except using dope, of course, because dope wasn't out then. But every other sin in the Book I'd been guilty of.

"I was discharged from the Army in November, 1945. I came back home, and though I was disinterested in church, I started going to church again—with my daddy and mamma, out of respect for them. In the spring of 1946 I was even elected song leader of the church! We just had sixteen members. My mamma played the piano and I could follow her playing and singing."

Raymond paused to chuckle. "Man! Those good old hymns that we had sung!

"During that summer we had a revival." He looked around at his listeners. "I don't know what you folks call a revival here, but it was a special week of services. We had an evangelist there preaching. One night, as he was extending the invitation, I was standing up there by the piano, singing, 'Just as I am, without one plea.' Just then the Holy Spirit spoke to me, the first time that he had ever. He convicted me then, that I was lost."

His voice softened. "But I was not ready to quit sinning at that time. But I did go over and take the preacher's hand and make a faltering dedication." He shook his head. "Well, of course, the Lord knew I wasn't ready, so by the next morning the conviction that had come the previous evening was gone.

"Right after World War II the G.I. Bill of Rights was passed that set up trade schools. Depending on the length of time you were in the armed services, a single man could get $65 a month, and go to school. Well, we managed to get a carpenter's class started in Whitewright, led by a qualified carpenter, and I entered that in 1947. My determination was to become a successful builder. Indeed, I finished my training within a year, and before long I was building houses. One night after I'd been out working hard all day, I was in bed asleep. I don't know what time it was—it was well past midnight, I'm sure. I woke up and in that half-conscious moment between asleep and awake, I saw this vision of myself standing up on a platform behind a pulpit. There were pews full of people sitting out there in front of me.

"I do not understand to this day why the Lord began to reveal to me about preaching when I was still lost. I don't suppose anybody has to explain why God does things. I guess he does them because he wants to. But, of course, I didn't want to preach! I was still going to be that successful builder. I never saw a vision that clearly before—but that one never did get away from me all that spring and summer. I'd go to bed after working hard nine or ten hours a day, tired, and lie on the bed, and toss and tumble with this problem of preaching.

"In August 1948 our Pastor and his wife left for China as missionaries. But just before they left some of our members said, 'We need some deacons.' Until then we only had one deacon, an old man who came to me and the Sunday-school teacher and asked us to consider being deacons. And so I was ordained as a deacon, though I knew full well I had no right to be one.

"But this urge to preach kept on until I made a statement at a prayer meeting one Wednesday evening. I said, 'Well, the Lord has called me to preach. I'm gonna have to give him my life for preaching.'

"Everyone in the church was happy, of course. They didn't know things weren't right. So they wrote me out a Certificate of Licence, and I went to Decatur, Texas, about a hundred miles away, and enrolled in the Decatur Baptist

College. Of course, our church let me preach right away when I told them I had surrendered to preach. When I came back home from college on weekends, I often used to preach. After the new Pastor arrived he called me long distance and asked if I would supply for him—because he had to be at the bedside of his father-in-law who was on the point of death with cancer.

"At that time the Baptist Convention of Texas employed some people to go out and work with small churches that needed help. They sent a worker for us out there at the church in Kentucky Town, for we were entering into a training and study course. There was a kick-off rally for that week of Training Union study in Denison, another one of the towns in our county. My sister and I took the lady worker from the Baptist Convention in our family car to the rally. We arrived early and four or five of the other lady workers were already there. A big pot-bellied preacher from out in West Texas was there, talking to the ladies, and he had the floor, of course. A preacher always has the floor, you know!"

Raymond chuckled softly, and went on. "I sat down on the bench on the opposite side where he was. Everything was so quiet that I could hear him plainly. Well, what he was telling those ladies was that he had been a Pastor out in Stamford, Texas, and that he had been invited by a friend from Southern Oklahoma one summer to preach a revival meeting. He said along of a Thursday night that week, after he had preached and the invitation was being extended, he was up in the pulpit. The Pastor was down on the floor, standing there, supposed to be receiving people that were coming. But the pastor turned around and came up to him and took him by the hand, and said, 'Preacher, I've never been saved!'"

Raymond took a deep breath and smiled. "Well, when he said that, I was looking over my shoulder to see if he was looking at me!

"After the service was over on Sunday night—the one in which I supplied for our Pastor—I met with the fellows that I was riding back to Decatur with. I was up there by the side of the driver, and he was quiet, driving, and I was just riding along there, minding my own business, when all of a sudden the Lord came and sat right down in that car with me."

Raymond's voice broke at the memory and he chuckled through his tears.

"He got right in my heart and began to disturb it. And I knew what was wrong just as soon as he started speaking to me. But oh! you don't know how stubborn some people can be—and I was one of them. I would not agree with him. I said, 'Oh, I'm just tired. I've had a busy weekend. I'll go home and get to bed, and tomorrow morning when I wake up everything will be all right.' After all, two years before that, when I'd been convicted one night, it was 'all right' in the morning.

"Well, it so happened on that Monday morning it wasn't all right." Raymond chuckled again. "And it didn't get all right—all day! Nor the whole week!

"But I was still not willing to come face to face with the thing. So I kept saying, 'When I go back home this weekend and go to church and see the folks again, it will be all right.'

"But at the weekend I drove up into my brother's yard first. He had three small children—a little son of about four, at the time, and two little girls that were older. When I got out of the car, they looked out of the door and they all came running: 'Oh, there's Raymond!' And they run out and grab me—and the Lord's voice was just like an arrow darting through me. The Lord said, 'Look at yourself! You're their preacher-uncle. They love you and respect you. But just look at yourself.'

"Well, I couldn't be happy there, so I went on home to my mother and daddy about a mile down the road. And here they come out on the front porch. Mamma grabbed me and hugged me. My daddy was a very soft-hearted man, tears rolling down…"

Raymond broke off, moved by the memory, dismissing his emotion with the usual chuckle.

"…and he took my hand. The Lord said again, 'Now look at yourself. Those old people love you. They've sacrificed for you. You're their preacher-son. Just look at yourself.'

"Well, I didn't like it! I didn't like what I saw at all. But I was still too stubborn to give in. So I tried to brush it off like I did before. But it wouldn't brush off. And when I got back to school the next Monday, that conviction had gotten so heavy, it seemed like there was a weight tied around my heart that weighed about a ton. I managed to get up to my room after lunch, and I fell face down on the bed.

"'Lord,' I said, 'what's wrong?'

"Of course, I knew—but he didn't hesitate. He said, 'You're lost.'

"'I know it,' I said, and went on: 'But look, Lord, I'm already here at school, a-preaching. What am I gonna do?'

"Well, strange as it may sound, he didn't tell me any specific thing to do. Instead, he put the three choices before me.

"'Well,' he said, 'you can go on as you are and be a hypocrite if you want to; or, you can just forget it and go back home and take up your carpenter tools and go to work; or, you can go back home and be a man and confess to the church what you are and get right.'

"'All right, Lord,' I said. 'That's what I'll do.'

"Well, of course, that burden lifted, because he had to see if I'd keep my word. But it was nearly two weeks till I got back home. By that time the devil had got his toe in the crack.

"'Now,' the devil reasoned, 'don't get carried away with this thing. You remember the experience you had in 1946?'

"'Yes, I remember.'

"'Well, don't you think you were saved then?'

"And I knew better, but I said, 'Yeah, I believe I was.'

"But my answer didn't seem like a good way out. So when I got back home, instead of doing what I should have done, I went before the church that Sunday and told them I had had an experience with the Lord—that I wasn't saved when I was a child, and that I needed to be baptised.

"Well, of course, they accepted that statement.

"When I went back to school on Monday, I thought I had been under some conviction and things would be all right now. But from that Monday morning until the following Friday night, I never experienced such conviction of sin as the Lord put upon me then. It felt like I was completely shut off from God, that there was no way to get to him. It was as though I'd committed the unpardonable sin! I began to pray out there yonder and in earnest:

"'Well, Lord, what can I do?'

"Every time I said, 'What can I do?', it was as if my words were hitting a brick wall and bouncing right back into my face:

"'What can I do, Lord? What can I do?'"

Raymond repeated the question, and each time struck the fist of the right hand into the palm of his left hand.

"'What can I do? What can I do?' But no answer came, and I kept struggling with it. I don't know how many times that week I saw myself seemingly out here..." He gestured with his right hand, indicating a high elevation. "...out here, on a tight cable stretched across a deep abyss down here that was full of fire and smoke." His left hand pointed towards the floor. "Now, I was suspended on that cable and I would think, 'Well, I guess I might just as well go up town and get me a gun and go into somebody's cow pasture and end it.'

"But when I thought that thought, I'd see myself being lowered into that pit of fire and smoke." He shook his head. "I can tell you for sure, folks, I expect that's probably the only reason I didn't commit suicide, because I was miserable.

"That Friday night, when I got home, they were having a cottage prayer meeting at our house for a thanksgiving revival. I met my sister in Whitewright and we drove out to the farm. We got out of the car and started towards the house, and got to the back porch; and, of course, mother met me. And you know mothers!"

He smiled as tears welled up in his eyes.

"She reached out and hugged me to herself. She put her hands against my chest and pushed me back and looked at me in my face." He chuckled. "I can still see it today!

"'Son,' she said, 'what in the world's the matter with you? Are you sick?'

"'No,' I said, 'there's nothin' wrong.'

"Mamma knew better than that! She didn't accept it at all. But after supper I took the car and went to get some people that wanted to come that didn't have a car and brought them there to that cottage prayer meeting. They asked me to lead—because I was a preacher. So I read a Scripture. Everybody around prayed. I went down on my knees and I went through the motion of saying a prayer too. When it was over I was ready to take those folks back home. When they were getting their coats on, I said, 'Well, I'll tell you, folks, before we leave here, I have a burden on my heart and I can't seem to get from under it. I wish ye'd pray for me.'

"Well, I don't know how many of them up and heard it; but when I'd got away from the house, I looked across over the way and the floodlights were on at the football fields at Whitewright.

"'Boy,' I said, 'that's what I need! I'll go to that football game when I get these folks home, and I'll get some relief and everything will be okay.'

"Well, when I got to the football game the half time was just beginning. They had a band, and they were marching out on the field to do their halftime activities. They had a boy that had one of those great big old bass drums hanging around his neck, and he was beating that drum! Ohh! I'm telling you, every time that stick hit that drum it felt like he was just pounding me right across the chest!

"When the second half started up, I walked round the front and sat down in the stand. But I made the mistake of sitting down next to the band position. When the band came back, there I was, right in the cheer-leading section. I found myself sitting right next to a girl who held a pair of brass cymbals. You know what those things are, don't you? When those cymbals crashed together, it was just like she was pounding the life out of me! I don't suppose I sat there five minutes. I couldn't stand it! And those guys out there playing football!"

He smiled. "Now, ordinarily, I can tell a little bit about football and what goes on on a football field; but on that evening it seemed it was like the mad cows trying to slaughter one another. So, I got in the car and just drove on back home, with all of this misery, saying to myself, 'Oh man, what can I do?' I had already quit praying, you see. I was fully convinced, all that drive home, that before daylight ever came I would be in Hell.

"When I drove in and parked the car, I got out and went into the house. Out there in that part of rural Texas, we didn't have electricity at that time, and used oil lamps. So I went into the dark, you know, real easy. I wasn't going to disturb anybody. I undressed and got into bed. That was somewhere between nine-thirty and ten o'clock, as near as I can give you the exact time.

"Now, as I snuggled myself into bed, pulled the covers up over myself, I remember that I said to the Lord, 'I've tried everything I can think of. I can't... there don't seem to be anything that I can do. So if there's anything that can be done, you do it.'

"Now, I hope I can say this clearly enough to get it good."

Raymond looked around at us and the tears welled up in his eyes. His next words thrilled us, spoken loudly, almost shouted, in a voice heavy with emotion:

"I SAW JESUS ON THE CROSS JUST AS PLAIN AS I CAN SEE ANYBODY HERE! I was looking up at his side; the blood was dripping from here, where the nails had pierced his hands."

Raymond pressed his right thumb into the palm of his left hand. His voice softened, but still trembled, as he went on.

"Down near his face were those crowns, where the thorns had pierced his brow. Blood was dripping from his feet, and from the gash—you know—where they had pierced his side with a spear. Well, that blood was running out and dripping on the ground there. And I was reaching up with all my strength, trying to reach up and just touch one of his toes. I thought, 'Oh, if I can just span the distance and touch him, it will be okay.'

"I could see the crowd of people back out here in a circle, who were spitting and mocking him. But out from behind the cross in the dark an Angel stepped out. He wore a long, white flowing robe that just barely swept the ground around his feet. It was a one-piece robe. And he had hair as black as jet—the prettiest hair I ever saw. And he held a teacup in his hand and walked right up between me and the Lord. He held that teacup right underneath that bloodstream; and when he had held it there an instant, he turned around and looked at me, and said, 'Now, will you accept it?'

"I said, 'Lord, pour it in!'

"His hand turned until that cup tilted at exactly the right angle and that blood all landed right here."

Raymond brought his large hand up against his breast.

"And I thought to myself right then, 'That...'—well, the devil put the thought there—'That couldn't be true.' But at that same instant something touched me on the side of the head. Then my mother's voice spoke and said, 'Son, has your burden been lifted?'

"'Yes, it has,' I said.

"And that's all that passed between us that night. I hadn't had much sleep, and she neither. When I got up next morning, after we'd had breakfast, she and I sat down in the dining room.

"'Well,' she said, 'would you like to tell me what happened?'

"'Yeah, I'll tell you,' I said, 'but I sure don't understand it.'

"But after I told her, she said: 'You know, I knew there was something wrong when you got home yesterday. And after you said what you did at the prayer meeting, I went to bed, praying for you. When I heard you drive into the yard, I was still praying. Soon after that I was still in such misery that I said, "Lord, I can't sleep tonight until I know that that boy's all-right." And the Lord said, "Well, why don't you get up and go and see?"'

"And so she got up and came. Then she put her hand on my head. I'm telling the full truth, folks, honest, it wasn't a split second's difference in the timing when that vision appeared and my mother's hand touched my head."

Raymond looked around at us. His eyes shone with the memory. It was real to him now as it was then.

"And," he continued, "when I lay down upon that mattress that night, I felt like I was so heavy I was going to press a hole through it right down through the floor and straight into Hell. But when that blood touched my heart, that terrible heaviness was all gone and it just seemed as if I rose off that bed and started floating in the air. Of course, I didn't actually leave the bed, but you know, I was so light.

And that bedroom was full of angels! There must have been ten thousand of them, just dancing and praising God!

"Well, I was too stunned for two or three days... I didn't know what to do. I kept saying to myself, 'Such things as this don't happen to anybody—like me. I've never heard of anything that would compare to that except the experience of Paul on the road to Damascus.' But the Lord kept me assured that it was real, all right. But then, whenever I begin to consider telling it to other people, the devil tries to get his argument in again. He says: 'You can't tell that. People won't believe it. They'll think you're crazy!'

"Well, I just had to get down to grips with it.

"'Lord,' I said, 'what about it? Do you think I really should tell it?'

"'Well,' he said, 'who gave you that testimony?'

"'You gave it, Lord.'

"'Okay, use it for me.'

"And that's what I've been trying to do—though I've failed a lot of times. I've been laughed at. A friend of mine that I grew up with—I tell you, I've wanted to see him saved—he had a church background and I told it to him. He looked at me like he'd been shot for just an instant, and then he just burst out in a horse-laugh.

"'Boy!' he said, 'you're just having wild dreams!'

"I went up to California, to attend the Golden Gates seminary there. The Pastor of the church where I was attending at this particular time asked me to speak one Sunday night, and I used my experience as the sermon—my full testimony just like I've given it to you here. When that service was over, he was standing at the door like a good preacher does, you know, shaking hands with the people as they went out. He took my hand, and he looked like he could throw a dagger through me. And he said: 'I just want you to know, I don't believe it!'

"'Well,' I said, 'My friend, I'm sorry. The Lord didn't make me responsible for you believing it. He just told me to tell it like it is. And that's all I'm doing.'"

Raymond Brown
Whitewright, Texas

HEAVEN'S GREATEST MIRACLE HAPPENED TO ME

Andrew Desouga

IT IS NOT BY CHANCE that you are reading this personal encounter of mine with GOD. You see, God told me to write it—you might say God spoke to *you*! Yes, you too can know the true and living God who can speak to you personally.

Once I did not know this living God personally. I was lost and I had no real hope and was without God, going my own way in the world. I was religious, going to church and carrying out the tradition, until I was confronted with the reality of sin in my life, and discovered that one day I would stand before a Holy God. I knew I had no chance of being with Him eternally.

About 32 years ago, I left my home in Kenya and arrived in England. Freed of restraints, I lived like many of my new friends. I was living with my girlfriend and in due course she became pregnant. Abortion was beginning to be popular at that time and it came to me that I would have been a murderer had such a thing taken place. It did not— but I realised I had done wrong and that I had ruined the lives of many people. I also knew that I had done wrong against God by disobeying His commandments. I looked for forgiveness. I was a Catholic so I went to Confession, and was told to repeat a few prayers and I'd be forgiven.

Perhaps the priest didn't take my sin as seriously as I did. I went to another priest but he said the same thing. I remember walking out and saying, "I want to meet this God personally—not just a man, but God—and I want to know who has the Power to forgive sins and who has the Authority to do it!" So I began to search.

My sister wrote from Kenya and told me Jesus could forgive my sins. Here I was in deep trouble and all she could do was talk about **JESUS!** When she came to England I eventually went along with her and her friends to a meeting. At first the talk of God's love and forgiveness angered me, but I kept going to the meetings.

I found it hard to believe that Jesus could forgive my sins. One day I was told to read the book of Romans in the Bible. When I started reading it, at first I thought, "Here is a man who knows all about philosophy." But reading on, I discovered that YES—Jesus has the authority and the power to forgive sins, my personal sins!

It became clear to me that as a sponge soaks up water, so had Jesus taken my sin and received the Judgement of the sin upon Himself on the cross, crucified for me, to set me free. What a demonstration of God's love! I saw, oh, how Jesus so loved me and you that He gave Himself a pure sacrifice in love for us.

But I had a problem—could Jesus forgive me after what I had done? I mean, this was such a big sin to me that I could not see how Jesus could forgive me for the terrible thing I had done. But then I realised, that if I didn't ask Jesus to forgive me, who else could I go to, as I had already searched elsewhere? I understood that Jesus had suffered for ALL my sins. My other problem was that if I did pray and commit myself to this God, to this Jesus, the Son of God, would He respond? I had been let down so many times before, and now to pray and trust all of my life to this God... how did I know I could trust Him? Would Jesus truly be real and respond to me personally?

My friends asked me if I had prayed and asked Jesus to be my Saviour. I said not yet, but I knew there was an urgency about making that decision—I *had* to pray.

That night, I knelt by my bed and though I could not see God, I prayed:

JESUS, I BELIEVE YOU ARE THE SON OF GOD, I BELIEVE YOU LOVE ME SO MUCH THAT YOU SUFFERED FOR ME, AND YOU DIED SHEDDING YOUR LIFE'S BLOOD ON THE CROSS FOR ME AND FOR MY SINS. I BELIEVE YOU ARE ALIVE, RESURRECTED FROM THE DEAD. PLEASE WASH ME OF ALL MY SINS IN YOUR PRECIOUS BLOOD. PLEASE FORGIVE ME FOR MY SINS, ESPECIALLY THE WAY THAT I HAD WRONGED MY GIRLFRIEND. COME INTO MY HEART, MY LIFE—I RECEIVE YOU AS MY SAVIOUR. MAKE ME A BRAND NEW PERSON LIKE YOU SAID YOU COULD MAKE ME.

That night, I had a vision. I was in a building and my friend said to me to go to another room because there was something there, so I went through a dark passage. I was kind of scared because of the dark. I entered an empty room and a rat ran along the skirting board and out of the room. Then suddenly, in the opposite corner of the room, I saw this dazzling white figure, absolutely pure white, brilliant, bright, and glorious—and I knew it was **JESUS.** I stood there as a dead man! I could not move or speak and from Him radiated rays of light and glory towards me, hitting my being, and things were fleeing from my chest. I could not understand what was happening to me.

When that was over, the Resurrected, Alive, Jesus walked up to me. He shook hands with me and spoke to me three times. He said, "Believe in God", and three times He said, "Believe in the Holy Spirit"—then the whole scene changed and miracles were happening in my sight. Jesus was communicating to me that with God nothing is impossible, and God can do the impossible. He is alive and does forgive the worst of sins.

When I woke up, I was crying and full of love for the first time. Something had happened to me. When I had gone to sleep, I was blind, and now when I woke up, I looked at the Bible beside me and, glancing at it, I knew what it was all about because the author had come to live in me! Hallelujah!

With His power in my life I was totally changed. I stopped smoking, drinking and swearing and I began to walk straight with the joy of the Lord, because I *knew* that I had met Jesus. He had forgiven me, He loves me personally, He knows me—He is real! I am a brand new man with the power of the Holy Spirit in me to live this life according to the Word of God.

This was the start of an eternal relationship with Jesus (27 years ago). It will never end. In this relationship, many wonderful things and miracles have happened to me and the people about me. Now I am not a stranger to God anymore and I would be so joyful to speak to you about this.

You do not need to wait for a miracle like this. In fact, as you have been reading this, Jesus has come near to you **in this very moment.** You see, God is Spirit, present everywhere.

You can pray the Prayer that I prayed, believe Jesus and mean it with all your heart and ask Jesus to forgive you all your sins, and Jesus will respond to you right now by actively forgiving you all your sins, blotting them out and washing you clean with His All-powerful Eternal living

Blood. Your hostile sins against God and man will be cancelled, never to be remembered by God or you—period! Because of Jesus, you have heaven's full legal right to be absolutely 100% forgiven and heaven forgets—that is, you have God's complete forgiveness. Heaven's blood shed by Jesus on the cross for you and me has wiped sin clean away already—it was done 2,000 years ago.

Don't be without this true knowledge and surrender to the unchanging wisdom of heaven. It is the wisest thing to do—surrender to the provision of God's unchanging *only way* of being forgiven. And yes! You also forgive others whatever bad things they might have done to you, even as Jesus did when they were crucifying Him. He said, "Father, forgive them for they know not what they do!" Surrender to God's personal character. Once sin is truly confessed God does not remember it any more—Jesus sets you free. What a heavenly glorious miracle, your guilt and burden carried away forever, to be remembered no more, and now to have God's peace with you, through Jesus' blood! With such glorious, active, powerful love for you, Jesus will respond instantly, forgiving you, and will come into your life the moment you truly ask Him—He will do it even right now.

The prayer that I prayed is the prayer of contact that connects you with Jesus when you pray. That's what happened to me when I prayed. In the vision I had, I walked down the passage to the heart of my life. In the vision, that dark room was my heart. I was serving a rat—Satan—who had made a mess of my life. As I prayed, that rat had to flee from my life and Jesus came into my life and lit up my heart with his light and glory and love. Now, CHRIST is in me and I am totally loved and fully accepted by God. Jesus' personal blood sacrifice guarantees my forgiveness and acceptance and has removed, abolished forever, the hostile barriers of my sin between God and me.

Jesus has given me His peace with God the Father, a living relationship. Imagine that, God the Father and His children bound together in love! Not only that, but also Jesus' living presence before God the Father guarantees and ensures the everlasting continuation of this supernatural miraculous reconciliation with God—Praise God! Thank God for Jesus! What a demonstration of His love extended to us. I know heaven is my home and God has become my Heavenly Father. I am loved by Him so much, and so are you very precious and so loved by Jesus. He cares for you. He has a plan for my life on this earth, and for you also, beginning with a new start in life with Jesus and with His power working mightily in you.

You NOW must ask Jesus to forgive you and receive Him into your heart and let Him light up your life so that you can see and be saved. **JESUS** is the only true hope— there is no other. Jesus said, "I am the way, the truth and the life, no man commeth unto the Father but by me" (John 14:6). *Let* heaven's greatest miracle of God happen to you personally: you too can have a daily living contact with Jesus. Hallelujah, and know and experience Jesus' personal merciful love and His forgiveness, forgiving you so that you too will also be a living miracle of God's mercy. You do not have to wait—*God cannot lie*, it is impossible for God to lie. He is not man, but God. It is not God's will for you to perish so *don't turn Jesus and His love away from you*: receive Him, don't be lost anymore, turn to Jesus and be found by Him and be saved and have a really meaningful life with Jesus. You really will be so glad— Jesus sets you free.

When you have talked to Jesus, or want to know more, go to the nearest Bible-believing church near you, or you can find me at Longmore Hall, Banff Road, Keith, Sunday 10.30 a.m. or 7 p.m.

Andrew Desouga
Drybridge, Scotland

THE ROCK OF AGES CLEFT FOR ME

Flo Pretorius

I LOOKED AT THE FRAIL FIGURE in the hospital bed. She was little more than a skeleton under the bedsheets. She was clearly in great pain and she had been coughing up blood for some time. The day before she had part of her intestine removed due to the spreading corruption of cancer. I could just make out the oval shapes of her eyes through the dark glasses she always wore. I bent close to her and put my hand on her soft grey hair.

"Flo." I tried to swallow the lump in my throat. "Flo, you can't go yet. I don't think your house is ready yet. The curtains must still go up."

She smiled. Her fingers barely managed to squeeze my hand.

"You know the Lord is always with you, Flo. Like the time he stopped the car going over the cliff. And when he took Gert off the ship. I've been praying for a long time. The Rock of Ages is cleft for you, remember?"

Her fingers tightened on mine. Her voice was just audible: "I know," she murmured. "Thank you."

* * *

Everyone in the Pietersburg Baptist Church loves Flo Pretorius. In spite of her creeping cancer, she has been an example of faith, patient acceptance and perseverance. Like her late husband Gert Pretorius, she is forever kind and gentle; and like him, she has never had a cross word for anyone. People are drawn to her, and find strength from her quiet acceptance of suffering, and from the obvious assurance and certainty of her salvation. She knows she belongs to the Lord and is forever secure in his presence. Because of her illness she looks older than 65. Yet, to know her is to love her, for she is a person of real beauty.

Her father had come to South Africa with the Connaught Rangers in the Boer War. He had married her mother, an Afrikaans girl from Lydenberg in the Transvaal. He returned with her to his native Somersetshire; but she wasn't happy in England, and so they came back to South Africa. They were the first white people to settle in Sekhukhune Land.

Flo was already in a very frail condition when my wife and I invited her to tea one morning. She was such an example of gentle love and patience that I asked her to tell me more about herself. This is the story she told me.

—*Charles Muller*

*   *   *

I grew up in Sekhukhune Land. My father used to say, "I wish you were always good like little red riding hood." I really thought I couldn't be as good as that, and one day I cut the shape of little red riding hood out of a blanket so I could hang it in my room. Oh, I got into such trouble for that!

But I wasn't really a naughty girl. Most of my early memories are of sitting on dad's knee while he told me about Jesus. Jesus soon became more real to me than little red riding hood!

Bishop Barker was a Catholic priest in Sekhukhune Land, and he took a keen interest in me, too. I was practically brought up in the convent. On Sundays I used to attend benediction in the morning and worshipped in the Anglican Church in the afternoon. It was like being brought up in two religions! But at the centre of either I felt close to the same Lord Jesus.

I was still very small when my mother became ill. It made me want to become a doctor. But I had to leave school to look after my mum. I can remember walking alongside the row of Pepper trees close to our home, feeling very lost. "Jesus," I prayed, "what's going to happen to me now?" Oh, I felt so very, very lonely! There was the rusty ruin of an old Chevrolet and the fowls scuttling in the dry heat. Yet Jesus was someone I already knew to be real, even there, in the heat and dust of Sekhukhune Land.

Oh yes, Jesus was always real to me! I suppose, just like a child does, you take things for granted. In a way I took Jesus for granted, because my father spoke of him so often. Jesus was someone I knew, just like my mother, or Bishop Barker. Except, of course, that Jesus was always there, even if you couldn't see him. I remember, one day, how the car daddy was driving started cooking on top of a mountain. He stopped the car on the steep road, but before we could get out it started to run back. Daddy pressed and pressed the brakes but it just kept running back. Then there was a soft thud as it came up against a rock. It was the only rock in the road. I remember how thrilled I felt when we got out and I saw it was only one rock that kept the car from falling down a precipice. I said, "Daddy, isn't it lovely that we love Jesus?" Daddy had often told me that the angel of the Lord camps about those who love him.

When I grew up I married Gert and we settled in the Cape. We had a lovely little boy with blue eyes. But he was only ten days old when Gert got orders to go North. It was during the second world war, and South African troops were sailing to North Africa to fight the Germans in the desert.

Gert was gone, and there I was with my small baby, and surrounded by strangers! Oh, I prayed and prayed! I said to the Lord: "I'm right down here in the Cape with my tiny baby. What's going to happen to us, Lord?" I never prayed so hard in all my life! Well, the Lord heard me, because three days later I received a telegram from Gert. It read: "Transferred to Lusikisiki, Transkei. Follow me."

When I stood on the Transkei coast arm in arm with Gert, I knew that God had answered my prayers. Gert had already embarked on the ship for North Africa when, for no apparent reason, a sergeant singled him out and ordered him to take up a position in the Post Office in Lusikisiki. Yes, he was taken off that boat! I watched the waves break against the rocks of the coast. There was one large rock with a bird right on top, just out of the reach of the foaming waves. Then the words of the hymn thrilled through me: "Rock of Ages cleft for me!" I knew God had cleft the rock for me, because of my prayers. Whatever happened, Gert and I would be safe from the angry waves of life.

And so, you see, my life was surrounded by God.

Lusikisiki was a small outpost—a trading post on the Wild Coast. The name Lusikisiki means "whispering of the reeds." You might say God's spirit was whispering in my life!

We went to the Dutch Reformed minister in Lusikisiki and asked him to baptise our little boy. The minister refused because Gert was in the army. So many Afrikaans people didn't support the war against Germany. So Gert said, "We'll go to the Anglican Church." And so the Anglican Church became our spiritual home for the next nine and half years. After that Gert was transferred to the Post Office in Bethlehem, in the Orange Free State. That was thirty-nine years ago. I can remember waving to the King and Queen when they drove through the main street!

Our little boy wasn't quite ten years old when we lost him. There had been a rugby match in Pretoria against the

All Blacks, and the cars were streaming home through Bethlehem. One driver had been drinking all day and barely knew what he was doing. My daughter Iona, who was two years younger than Andy, was standing near him next to a tree by the roadside.

"Andy, watch out!" she shouted in horror.

But it was too late. The car threw him fifty yards. The impact burst his heart and his liver. We just saw him flying through the air. We thought it was the dog. But it was our own dear child! It was such a shock we didn't feel it at first. Even when Gert picked up his lifeless body and carried him out of the gathering crowd—we just couldn't believe it had happened.

It took us a really long time to realise that our child had been killed. He had been a real little angel, with his fair curly hair and blue eyes. He was a little gentleman, kind and loving, and would often come to you and put his arms round you. Strangers would put their hands on his head and say, "What a beautiful child!" He used to look after the watches of the school boys playing rugby, wearing them all along his arm. Iona used to complain, "Mummy, people always take notice of him and not of me!" The day after he was killed a parcel arrived from my mother, full of jerseys she had knitted for him. I gave them all to the local mission station and I thought my heart would break.

But the Rock of Ages was still cleft for us and somehow God kept us out of the reach of the angry waves. Gert didn't hold any grudge against the driver of the car, who also had a wife and children. "There's no point in making life more miserable for them, too," he said. The Methodist minister who conducted the funeral service also consoled us greatly. "God doesn't always want the flowers that are open," he said. "He wants the buds, too."

There was a court case because the State prosecuted the driver, and little Iona was called as a witness in court. She stood on the witness stand and said in a clear voice, "My mummy says I must tell the truth and nothing but the truth!" Everyone clapped and someone gave her five shillings. The judge was very impressed by her impartiality, too—but he sentenced the man, nevertheless, to a year's imprisonment and took his driver's licence away for two years.

Life isn't meant to be a bed of roses, of course. Even tragedy can be important, for it makes one strong. We are all of us vessels in God's temple, and He wants to mould us for his service. I remember telling that to a grumpy old man in the hospital where I worked as Matron. He grumbled over everything, and all day long, too. He didn't like the food, or the way his bed was made. "You're in for the high jump!" he said if we didn't come promptly when he called. He was such a rude old man. He just wanted to break everyone. Once he even threw his tea onto the floor.

"You ask for tea and you get dishwater!" he shouted.

"You know, Mr Hector," I said, keeping my cool. "Did you ever realise that Jesus didn't have a pillow to lay his head on?"

He turned his aggressive eyes on me but didn't say anything.

"Had you ever thought of that?" I insisted.

He stared at me for a long time. Then he conceded in his gruff voice: "No, Matron. I never thought of that."

Oh, I brought that cross old gentleman to the Lord! He changed his life completely. No-one could believe it. He became polite and actually smiled at the nurses. He even apologised for his former rudeness! I felt so happy that I got the man to change his whole life. It was the Lord, of course, that did it. But it was just saying those few words that gave the Lord the opportunity!

I've still got to better myself in so many ways, and I just ask God to keep me on the right road. But life has always been a matter of going forward, of becoming a little more like Jesus every day. You can't be like the Dead Sea, just receiving and going stagnant. You've got to give, too, and the more you give of yourself the more the fresh water of God's spirit flows in. I remember one old lady in hospital whose life was an example of love and patience. We all thought she was going to die. But she knew her time hadn't come yet. She smiled and told us: "My heavenly home isn't finished yet. The curtains still have to be hung."

Gert and I settled in Pietersburg seven years ago. We went to the Baptist Church and it was the first sermon the young minister preached, for he had just come to Pietersburg, too. He preached on the text from John 14: "In my Father's house are many mansions... I go to prepare a place for you... that where I am, there you may be also." Gert enjoyed it and I just loved it. "Now I've found what I want," Gert said.

Soon after that the doctors found that I had cancer. I went through two operations and grew more and more frail. Everyone prayed for me, of course, and I suppose they expected me to die long before Gert. He went to the evening service alone one Sunday and came back very tired. "I'm so tired," he said. "I should really have stayed at home tonight." When he was sipping his tea he said, "You know, if anyone didn't come to the Lord after that service...!" The minister had said that only by grace can we come to Jesus, and had spoken of Jesus coming back soon. "Who knows," the minister—the Rev. Mike Taylor—had said to the congregation, "perhaps the next time I see you will be in the Kingdom of God!"

When I woke the next morning my beloved Gert was dead. At the funeral service the young minister recalled the concluding words of his sermon. Yes, the next time we would see Gert would be in the Lord's Kingdom. I praise God that we are covered by the Lamb's blood and that we shall meet again!

My cancer has grown steadily worse and I may not come through the operation next week. But there are so many people praying for me, I don't see how I cannot come through! Anyhow, I had a lovely dream last week. I dreamt I was in heaven and I saw this beautiful lake with building plots and half-completed houses all around it. There were libraries and parks, but best of all the Saviour was there, watching and taking care of everyone!

I wonder if my house is ready? It might just be the curtains that have to be hung.

Flo Pretorius

* * *

Flo's house in heaven wasn't ready yet. In fact, shortly after her operation she moved into a brand new flat in Pietersburg, where she put up pretty beige curtains with patterns of green flowers.

STRENGTH MADE PERFECT IN WEAKNESS

P C Mokgokong

FROM MY POSITION on the stage I could clearly see the Vice-Chancellor. He sat in his wheelchair and transfixed the assembly with hooded eyes that expressed a mixture of love and amusement. The fact that he had no legs barely detracted from his sense of presence. Academic gowns of burnished gold and scarlet rustled as the professors and heads of departments settled into their seats.

The background music subsided and the Vice-Chancellor's voice filled the auditorium. It was the 1985 graduation ceremony of the University of the North, and he welcomed the graduands and their parents. "We welcome the media, too," he said, and added with a Churchillian air, "Provided, of course, that their reports are positive!"

He went on to speak about the time of crisis through which South Africa was passing. "But we will pass through the sticky patch," he said. His stentorian voice expressed total certainty. "Even if we have to limp along! We will reach our goal for a new and ideal University in the year 2000! When I launched the project PLAN UNIVERSITY OF THE NORTH 2000 in 1981, I foresaw the need to restructure this University to serve the changing needs of the communities in which it stands. Having set our goals, we don't look back. We only look forward!"

Yes, I thought. He wasn't a man to look back. The second black Rector of the University, he had proved himself a capable leader even before he had lost his legs. And now he dealt with crises as a matter of daily routine. Just three weeks ago a body of angry students had swarmed into his home, chanting and upsetting chairs. They demanded the dismissal of certain members of the white staff, including all those with the name of 'Botha,' the name of the State President. Even then the Rector's presence, reduced to the level of his wheelchair, withered the towering rage of the angry young men. "I don't negotiate with a mob!" he had said, and one by one they had dropped their eyes and left the room.

It was only the previous year, in 1984, that the Rector had come through the worst crisis of his life. A diabetic disease had left him no alternative to amputation, and I had wondered how he had managed to face that crisis. I went to see him, determined to find out the source of his strength. It was in the study of his campus home that he told me the story of his triumph. The following is his testimony.

—*Charles Muller.*

* * *

My brother, who is a medical professor at MEDUNSA (the Medical University of South Africa), came to see me last year. He had heard that my illness had worsened and was anxious to make a personal diagnosis. When he arrived he saw instantly that my condition was critical. He said I would have to be taken to the hospital at once. By the time he had me in the car he had already phoned a team of surgeons who were standing by. He spoke to me as a doctor, not a brother. He said, "There's no other cure but amputation." His words chilled me and I was very afraid.

When I arrived at the hospital a British surgeon, Dr Cotton, considered my general condition to be too weak for the operation. I was treated with drugs for three days. When

I went into surgery, I had little desire to face it and had almost lost the will to live. I was semi-conscious, after the operation, for six days.

On the seventh day I came to my senses, still feeling confused. I looked about me and said, "Where am I?" By sheer coincidence—was it really coincidence, I wonder?—Professor Van Wyk, the surgeon who performed my operation, was at that moment walking by and heard my words. He swung round, very excited, and took me out of the intensive care unit. Then he sat down on my bed and smiled. His words thrilled me with their obvious emotion: "You've made it!" Coming from him, a stoic and businesslike surgeon, his heartfelt exclamation was like manna from heaven. Then Dr Cotton came in, happiness and relief spread over his face, too. "Thank God you didn't wait another seven days before coming to us," he said softly. "You'd be dead, otherwise." I think it was the joy of seeing the caring concern of these men that touched me. They really wanted me alive!

It was after that that I began to read. A friend brought me two books—*Champion's Story*, by Bob Champion and Jonathan Powell, and *Faith is the Answer* by Norman Vincent Peale. I found *Champion's Story* thrilling, about the courage of a man who went on to win the Grand National after being a cancer patient. I read the book in one day.

But Norman Vincent Peale's book really moved me. It led me to the Bible where I found immense comfort in the unsurpassable love and strength of God. I couldn't ask for my leg back, of course. But God said, "My grace is sufficient. My strength will be made perfect in weakness" (2 Cor. 12:9). It didn't matter, anymore, that I had less strength, or *seriti*, which is the Sotho term for personal power or spirit. I could surrender to the power of the Almighty. My weakness—or my disability—was like a precondition for that illimitable Strength of God.

After a weak Professor Van Wyk examined my remaining leg. He shook his head.

"It's not responding to treatment," he said.

"You'll have to take it off, then," I said.

He looked up in surprise. "You don't object?"

I smiled. "You're the doctor. Whatever you say."

I was just following me medical routine, as far as I was concerned. More weakness, in a physical sense, meant more strength from God. His strength would be made even more perfect in my weakness.

The leg was removed the following morning. Later, on the same day. I was talking to my visitors. They were amazed by my cheerfulness, by my casual acceptance of the inevitable, and by the obvious strength of my constitution so soon after the operation.

We are going through difficult times of change and readjustment in South Africa, and I frequently have to deal with unrest on the campus. My role as arbitrator and peacemaker, and as instigator of change, too, is not an enviable one. Sometimes I have to make a firm stand — against student demands, and even staff demands. Running a university from a wheelchair in a time of crisis is certainly a new challenge. And I've heard it said, jokingly, that 'the Rector, now that he has no leg to stand on, puts his foot down!'

What many don't realise, of course, is that I'm plugged into the Spirit power of the Universe. And I praise God that He is the constant source of my strength.

P C Mokgokong

TAPPING INTO THE SPIRIT

Charles Muller

Come near to God, and He
will come near to you.
(James 4:8)

ABOUT 4 A.M. on the 28th of November, 1984, I had
a strange and wonderful experience. In essence, I told
God I loved him—and to my amazement, he answered me
and told me he loved me.

That was it, in a nutshell; but the experience was so
shattering I don't think I'll ever be the same. I've told
people it was like an extra-terrestrial experience, because I
had never experienced anything like it before. However,
before I go into details about it, I'll need to say something
about the events that led up to it. The experience, you see,
came as the climax of a year of seeking and doubt.

I suppose I'd always felt there would be something
special about 1984. Perhaps it was because of George
Orwell's novel *Nineteen Eighty-Four!* But it was special
for me because it was my sabbatical year. My previous
sabbatical leave was seven years earlier in 1977, the year I
met my wife Jo. This time it meant a whole year off from
the university in South Africa where I was employed as a
professor of English. At last, I would be able to complete
my long-cherished book on the Christian teachings of
Charles Kingsley, the Victorian novelist. But it also meant
that, in the acres of free time, I would be able to finish
writing my novel based on the second-coming of Christ. It
was a novel I was writing with Jo, and we had decided to

call it *Rapture at Sea*. (In the book Jesus is seen to come back early one morning while a ship is traversing the stormy waters of the Bay of Biscay; imagine the consternation of the passengers when they discover all the Christian passengers have vanished! The novel was finally published under the pen-name Carolyn Charles.)

At any rate, writing a novel would be a refreshing change to writing academic articles and textbooks. In a way, I had had a surfeit of academic writing, with eight published textbooks and three doctorates behind me. Much of it had been for my own glory, and I felt I had never fulfilled my real purpose for the privilege of being in this world—to proclaim God's word and his glory.

There was another aspect of the year which had little to do with glorifying God. It was the year when I bought my Rolls-Royce. I had long cherished the notion of acquiring what people term 'the best car in the world.' Well, why not? I had worked hard, writing textbooks, and had travelled repeatedly to the tropical outposts of my university to lecture in conditions of sweltering heat. But at heart, of course, I was seeking a cherished desire.

And so, for various reasons, I chose to spend the year in Britain. Jo is British and she longed to spend time in a setting that was green and exhilarating like the Yorkshire dales where she had roamed free as a child. We needed a secluded spot for our writing. And, of course, Britain was the home of many Rolls-Royce cars.

We found the perfect place: a cottage at the head of a secluded glen just south of Oban in Scotland. In the winter it was a bleak glen and Scammerdale Loch looked forbidding with its dark waters, waves ridging across the surface as the wind whined around us. The cottage was warm and cosy with its oil-fired central heating. The windows gave panoramic views of the loch, fringed by the Christmas pines and mountains that opened to the amorphous sky. We watched the snow settling on the mountaintops while the rain filtered down gently, soaking everything. The cottage was like a life-support capsule, a micro-world set in this wonderful yet alien environment of cold, snow and drizzle. We observed the world in safety, like seeing the landscape of a strange planet from the security of our capsule.

'It's lovely,' Jo said. She looked wistful, her deep brown eyes raised to the powdered peaks above.

'It *is* bleak, though.' I looked up at the sky. 'Look how dull it is.'

'Yes, but the atmosphere is tremendous.' She frowned. 'It's dull, yet the sky retains light. There's a feeling of hope and contentment. Listen to the wind. There's music in it.'

'That moaning noise!' I laughed.

'No, I like it. The place has a feeling of warmth, of home.' She smiled. 'Perhaps this is as close to heaven as I'll get on earth.' Then she turned to me, concern in her eyes. 'You know, I don't want this year to pass. It holds my future, somehow.'

I suppose, in a sense, it did hold her future. If our writing partnership proved successful, it meant the possibility of writing full time and settling in Britain where she most wanted to live. Somehow she sensed, I think, that I wasn't altogether with her in spirit. I wanted to write a novel, yes—but there was the Rolls Royce, too, and that meant taking all our British money back with us to South Africa. For me, the Rolls Royce was like a golden calf and demanded a sacrifice.

Looking back, the year was full of vivid impressions. It turned out we had chosen the worst winter in twenty years. The snow fell and fell and heaped up in drifts a few feet thick. One day Angus, the farmer next door, came churning up to the cottage in his four-wheel drive. The school car with our young children in it hadn't returned, and the snowstorm was turning into a blizzard with winds over 70 mph. We found the car, all right, bogged down in a drift next to the loch. The little faces of the children were white and anxious as they peered through the windows, but relieved to see us.

The gale swirled the snow around us as we dug around the tyres. Our hands grew numb and our movements sluggish. I felt like a man of soaked cardboard pretending to dig. The shovel weighed a ton and around me was the swirling white, blinding to look at. The frightening thing about a blizzard is that the whole world 'whites out.' If I stepped more than a few feet away from the car I could see nothing at all—just blinding whiteness.

The car and the children were safely rescued, at any rate. But the memory of the occasion lingers with me, like a lesson. It reminds me that we can't step too far back from Jesus, or we'll lose sight of him. We would be swamped by chaos. Somehow we have to keep him in sight, and our eyes on him. Just like Peter walking on the water: as long as he kept his eyes on Jesus and not on the waves around him, he didn't sink.

My most vivid impression, of course, was acquiring the Rolls Royce. (One doesn't 'buy' a Rolls, a salesman in Glasgow told me: one 'acquires' one.) It was magnificent, of course, long and sleek in gold over walnut. The children were quite enthralled, being driven out of London in such a magnificent dream machine. Yet this was one experience I could have done without. Even the Saturday traffic in London was heavy, and I kept losing my way as I tried to find the M1 out of London. I was terribly tense manoeuvring so expensive a piece of technology through unknown streets of speeding vehicles. I was barely in the right frame of mind to thrill at the superb handling, the gliding motion, the finger-sensitive steering, the silent and powerful thrust of the engine as it propelled us into traffic streams. But at last we surged into the freedom of the motorway, relaxing as we adjusted our seats for maximum comfort, feeling ourselves lift and tilt as little electric motors hummed discreetly. For a moment I was transported—more than literally, I mean! The realities were cushioned and translated into a new 'spirit' existence. The wet windscreen, the wipers moving intermittently, insulated me from a world that was familiar but distanced.

It was fun, for a while, owning a Rolls Royce. It was difficult to justify, though, and I tried to see it as an unavoidable part of my destiny. In a way, I had made it a part of my destiny, of course. In March I wrote in my diary:

Destiny is irresistible, and may seem illogical. It seems illogical for me no—at this point in my life—to buy (I mean acquire!) a Rolls Royce. But there it is—it demands obedience and expression now. The Rolls Royce from henceforth is a vital expression of my life. To avoid it is to ignore an obsession, and that would damage my creativity.

But, really, I was feeling more than a little guilty for having spent so much money on a personal ambition. And it wasn't long before a certain dryness of heart set in.

I felt a need to get closer to the Lord. The novel was finished and by the summer had already been rejected twice by publishers. Jo and I began our next novel, which we called *Spirit of Ecstasy* after the Rolls-Royce mascot. (This novel was a romance and featured the Rolls in the story; but it was really about an academic who, like myself, feels dissatisfied with life and misguidedly buys a Rolls Royce in search of spiritual fulfilment. Again, this novel was published under the pen-name Carolyn Charles.)

I began to climb up into the hill above the cottage to seek more guidance from God. I found a tree growing out of a slope, and the trunk was looped to form a perfect seat. Sitting there, overlooking the loch, now an expanse of deep blue set amongst soft green slopes, I felt close to God. The breeze caressed the leaves above me and the white dots of sheep on the slopes added to the tranquillity of these moments. There I sat, reading daily from Psalm 104, about God who 'makes the clouds his chariot' and 'walks upon the wings of the wind.' The evidence of what I was reading was all around me. I had once discovered this third verse of Psalm 104 on a stone plaque in the Valley Gardens in Harrogate, in 1977. It had given me comfort then, and soon afterwards I had had a marvellous experience of divine reassurance in the wind sweeping through the trees in Wolloton Park. So now, again, I was seeking comfort—and reassurance.

'Dear Lord,' I prayed. 'Use our writing to your Glory. That's all that I really want. Publish our novels, and I will use them as a platform for preaching your Gospel.'

Was it a kind of a bargain with God? In any case, he ignored these prayers. The manuscript of *Rapture at Sea* kept coming back from publishers. The theme was too esoteric or way-out, they said.

Eventually I became fed up. Jo could no longer help me write, either, since she was having trouble with her eye. She had got a seed stuck in her cornea, but our doctor in Oban thought it was an infection. He kept prescribing ointments and the problem persisted for three months. Eventually the impediment was removed at the hospital in Glasgow. Nevertheless, before then, the sense of darkness and failure grew stronger, in spite of a beautiful summer.

'Dear Lord,' I prayed. 'Please heal Jo's eye. And don't forget the novel.'

But he remained silent. The summer slipped by and the sense of failure increased.

'The whole year is a waste of time,' I said bitterly, one day, as we sat beside the stream that fed the loch.

'How can you say that?' Jo squinted at me through her dark glasses. Because of her eye she couldn't stand the light.

'Time is supposed to be growing short before the Lord returns. How can we spread the Gospel if we can't find a publisher?'

'You're so impatient.' Jo waded into the stream, keeping her face turned away from the sun as she tried to catch a minnow. She was enjoying Scotland, in spite of her eye. 'We have to serve our apprenticeship first. People don't publish their first novels.'

But in spite of her sensible advice, I grew angry with the Lord. He seemed to ignore my prayers. What was the point of going up into the mountain? The year was drawing in, in any case, and it grew colder and windy again. Soon I stopped speaking to the Lord altogether. I didn't bother with the Bible, either. I got on with my Kingsley project, visiting universities and libraries in the south. I barely gave the Lord a thought.

One dark night I felt particularly depressed. The year had almost completely wasted away, and all I had to show for it was a Rolls Royce that gave me little satisfaction. I walked out into the night and once again spoke to the Lord.

'Lord,' I said, leaning on the cold metal of a farm gate. 'Frankly, I don't think you're there.'

I felt idiotic, speaking into what I knew was a void.

'I don't feel anything, God.' I listened to the stillness of the night, hoping there would be some sign of his presence.

Some dark shapes moved in front of me, restlessly, and I caught my breath. But they were just cows. I felt cheated, spending all this time writing novels for his glory. What did he care?

'In fact, God, I…I don't think you really care.' I grew more daring. 'In fact, I don't think you really exist.' It was the first honest prayer I had prayed for a long time. 'I don't *feel* anything. Surely, in your great power, you could make me feel something, if you cared?' It was a challenge, I suppose. I listened, trying to feel something. But there was nothing. I was praying into a vacuum.

'Anyway, God, I'll go on talking to you. Just in case you *are* there.'

I listened again. This time...yes, this time I *did* hear something. It was like soft footsteps in the night. The grass rustled nearby. I held my breath. Had he really heard me?

The grass near my feet moved and a black cat slunk past me. It disappeared into the night.

I felt drained and flat. 'You see, God,' I said, 'I even hoped that cat was you.' I turned away and walked disconsolately back to the cottage.

Just after that a book arrived unexpectedly from Ruth and John, Christian friends living in Cape Town. The book was *Nine o' clock in the Morning* by Dennis Bennett. I threw it aside when I saw it was about the work of the Holy Spirit. Later, however, I began to dip into it, and found that Bennett frequently asked the Lord for small things — and got answers, too. If he wanted a dry day for a picnic, for instance, he would ask the Lord to stop the rain from falling in the picnic spot he planned to use; *and* he would find, when he got there, that it was the only spot for miles where it *w*asn't raining.

That was odd, I thought. And yet, if the Lord really cared, he *would* show his concern in small things.

So I thought I would ask for silly things, too—things which nevertheless mattered to me.

One of the things that was on my mind was a new stainless steel exhaust system I wanted fitted to the Rolls Royce before it was shipped to South Africa. I had arranged with a small specialist in Yorkshire to do the job on a certain Monday a week before the shipping date. It was the only day he could do the job, but he warned me that he couldn't do it if it rained. He was good at supplying and fitting new exhausts, but had to do it in a yard where there was no cover. 'I'll have to arrange for a dry day, in that case,' I said.

So I approached God again. 'Lord,' I said, 'I know this is very silly. But I do need to have that exhaust fitted on Monday. And you know I can't afford the more expensive garages. Could I have a dry day on Monday? Just in Boroughbridge, that is. You can let it rain everywhere else.'

When Sunday came and we were driving the Rolls southwards to Yorkshire, there was a disturbing smell of burning mingled with the sumptuous aroma of leather. I couldn't locate it, and I eventually asked the Lord to show me where it was coming from. At once smoke appeared from under Jo's seat and she gave a shout of surprise. I stopped the car and found the old exhaust had developed a hole and was blasting hot gasses up at the floor of the car, baking the carpet! I telephoned the Automobile Association from the next service stop and they were on the spot at once. They flattened a beer can and wrapped it around the pipe. This must have been the first time a Rolls was patched with a beer can!

The next day, of course, was my appointment in Boroughbridge in Yorkshire. I found the place on the Sunday evening in the rain, just to make sure I knew where to go the next day. I found the man and said, 'It's raining.' He said, yes, the forecast was bad for the whole week, but he told me to bring the car to him the next day anyway: he would just have to cope.

The next day dawned and the leaden clouds hung ominously in the sky. But for the whole day, not one drop fell! And the new exhaust system was fitted expertly.

Two days later I had another appointment, this time in Luton near London for a new windscreen. (I wanted a tinted windscreen fitted before shipping the car.) There had been forecasts of serious fog. The week before there had been a terrible pileup on the motorway due to fog. 'Please Lord,' I prayed, 'I'd rather not have fog.' When the day came the winter sun shone brilliantly on the motorway. I put on the radio of the car, just in time to catch the announcer's warning: '...motorists to drive with extreme care in the terrible weather at present lashing the country…' *What* terrible weather? The day was calm and the sun was actually being a nuisance!

So I came, eventually, to accept that it didn't matter about *feeling* in one's relationship with God.

'The Lord is a FACT,' I said to Jo. 'His presence is a fact. He is real and unquestionably *there*. That's all that matters.'

'Yes.' Jo looked at me with amusement. She had been to Glasgow hospital by this time so she could look at me with both eyes. 'But one should feel God's existence, too.'

'No,' I insisted. 'Feeling doesn't matter. It's enough that he exists!'

It was important, of course, that each day I was getting one step closer to God. I was spending more time in prayer, again, because now I knew he was listening — even if I didn't feel anything.

Just after that I was alone in London for a final visit to the British Library. The car had been shipped and in two weeks we would all be on our flight back to South Africa. It was the 27th of November and a British Council friend kindly put me up in his London home. He gave me a comfortable bed in a tiny room at the top of his house. I was hardly prepared for the incredible surprise in store for me.

It was about four the next morning when I woke up with some asthma. I turned over and lay on my back when I became aware of a woman seated beside my bed. I ought to have jumped out of my skin, especially since she radiated a soft light! But the strange thing was I wasn't in the least bit frightened. On the contrary, there was an immense sense of peace and warmth and contentment. And, I *knew* her — or, I should say, it was as though my spirit recognised her. Yet I couldn't put a name to her. It didn't matter. It was enough that she was there. She was elderly, and I felt afterwards she was like an old German teacher I was very fond of as a child. But afterwards (and this is very strange, for I don't understand it) I felt she was like Corrie ten Boom: that name came to me very clearly, afterwards, yet at the time I had never read any of her books. In any case, the sense of warmth and comfort made me want to pray. I lay back and said, simply: 'God, I love you.'

That was when it happened. All at once there was a flood of light from above: a sudden downpour, like an energy beam of pure power and pure love. It came straight down, like a pillar from heaven: but it was a stream of heavenly power, like electricity that surged through me, like a waterfall pouring, rushing through me.

I knew it was God. It was overwhelming. I felt like a small child on the breast of its father, held ever so tightly. I was crying and sobbing helplessly, overcome with joy. Somehow it was my spirit that was crying, not my physical body. I was held in a firm grip: movement was impossible. I had closed my eyes, and now I dared to open them for a moment: the room was flooded with light! A vague human form stood by the bed. I felt fear, yet total acceptance by God: it was too much for me to stand for long. I wish I'd had the courage to surrender totally to the accepting love of God. And I felt so unworthy, so ashamed, in spite of the total acceptance by God. Perhaps that's why I cried: 'Oh, please, please let my life be worth something to you!' And yet no demand was being made on me. At that instant, very powerfully, I felt the sentences in my mind, wordlessly, like a telepathic force: 'It's all right. You don't have to justify yourself or do anything to make me love you or want you.'

Then suddenly it was all over.

But as I thought, 'It's over,' and while I still felt elated from the experience, I was aware of a desk standing in the room. It was a visual impression, of course, but the physical reality of the desk was uncanny and lucid. It was a modern desk, tall and narrow, like a pulpit. It felt inviting. I knew then that my calling was to write — to proclaim

God's word and message of love through the written word. As if to confirm this, the thought pressed into my mind: 'Feed my lambs.'

And then, finally, there was a feeling, like a chuckle, as though God were saying, 'Did you say feeling didn't matter?'

That was years ago, but I still ask, 'Did it really happen?' Of course, I know it did. I've been blessed with more than biblical proof that God lives and that he loves me too! For some time after the experience I had an overwhelming sense of love for everyone that I never had before.

Since then I've read Corrie ten Boom's *Tramp for the Lord*. She describes a similar experience of the Lord's presence—when she was healed in hospital. In a sense, I was healed, too. God goes to the sinners and failures, and I was failing badly.

Charles Muller
Stirling, Scotland

A STRANGER AND A DOG

(Written by the Rev Dr Louis Bosch as told to him by Dennis Leisegang, October/November 2000 in The Grande Restaurant, Rosebank Mall, Johannesburg, in South Africa.)

THE FARMERS in the Sterkriver community west of Potgietersrus in the Northern Province of South Africa had arranged one of their very popular parties. The party was to take place in a suitably decorated barn where the occasion could best be enjoyed in the fullest and earthiest manner! Dennis Leisegang, a bachelor farmer in the area, decided to go although he tended to be a recluse rather than one given to wild hedonistic social endeavours.

He was not particularly religious, although he did attend the Methodist Church in the area. This was the mid-eighties and he had other ideas about his future and about what mattered as far as spiritual things were concerned. His decision to go was because of feeling somewhat down. He felt the need to get out and try to "lighten up" a bit. Things, generally speaking, had not been easy on the farm and certain relationships had also added to the unsettledness, the restlessness and the feelings of depression that flooded over him from time to time.

Came the night of the party, he found himself on his way there, quite unaware of anything being out of the ordinary. He joined a table of familiar faces and some friends and, with a sense of reckless abandon, was prepared to enjoy what the evening brought. As the party began, so began the enjoyment of freely flowing drinks, good things to eat, the music and the eroticism of men and women happy to be together and happy to be dancing with the hope that some dream or some promise would come to fulfilment as the evening followed its course of ever growing liberty and chatter.

After a while Dennis offered to go to the bar and get something to drink for himself and his friends. So he took their orders and went over to the bar. While waiting to be served he turned to look at the crowd. He knew so many of them, and as he looked at them, wondered about them—who they really were, what they felt deep down, and what they really wanted out of life. He thought it a little strange, thinking like this and at such a time, and then thought nothing more of it.

Then it happened.

As he watched the crowd he felt a strange warmth he couldn't grasp, nor understand, begin to flow through him from head to toe. It was as if some kind of light surrounded him and a waterfall of what he could only term overwhelming love poured over him. It was flooding him, so to speak, and he couldn't help himself as he succumbed to this feeling of love, a tremendous welling up within him, probably from this outpouring that flooded over him. It was an overwhelming love for all those he could see in the well of the barn before him.

He felt weak, a little faint, and knew he had to get out into the open air as the experience seemed to settle over him and within him. In his mind this was far too weird to explain and somewhat frightening to entertain in his thoughts. He left the order for the table and went outside not only for air but to try and understand, to come to terms with what was happening to him. The sense of the "light" and the glow of the warmth was still with him as he passed through the doors into the open air. It was still quite light outside and he felt he needed to walk.

As he stood outside of the barn he could see the farm dam with its wall about four hundred meters slightly to his right; further to his right he could see the grove of trees and bushveld, about three hundred meters from the dam. It presented a triangle he felt would be a good distance for a walk that would provide the air he needed. All this time the feelings he had experienced still glowed and flowed around him and within him.

He had not gone too far from the barn when he sensed he was being followed. He turned to see a young couple some thirty meters behind him, following him, and he concluded they were probably out to get some air as well. Potgietersrus could be an uncomfortably hot place.

Dennis walked slowly, his mind filled with whirling thoughts as he tried to come to terms with the tremendous feeling of love he was experiencing. He was not particularly religious, but, could this be some sense of Call or visitation, he wondered? The man and woman behind him were forgotten as he walked slowly and contemplatively along the pathway he had chosen.

He passed the dam and from time to time thought he felt the couple looking towards him. This was a further puzzle to him. Why should they appear to be so interested in him? He found himself heading towards the grove of trees and bush which now appeared to be much darker and rather still. Slowly, he came to the grove, his thoughts no clearer, his feelings still unexplained: he sensed within him that something had possessed him, had filled him with the love which still flooded within and over him.

Then, as he approached the grove, a large Bull Mastiff came out of the trees and made straight for him. He stopped, wondering what this huge dog would do, for he knew these dogs were vicious and were used on the farms for all sorts of reasons -- for guarding, protection, even killing. He stood, eyeing the dog and waited. He had no idea what the dog would do.

The dog walked straight to where he stood and simply nudged his hand that hung loosely at his side. Then it turned and disappeared into the grove and bush. Dennis was surprised, nonplussed, never expecting this. He stood trying to make sense of this and all that was happening to him. What was going on? What did all this mean?

Bemused by the strangeness of it all, Dennis was standing very still when he became aware of the couple that had been following him. They were standing a few meters from him, transfixed. He looked at them and saw they had obviously been frightened by something terrible. Their eyes were wide with fear and, even in the increasing darkness as the night drew in; he could see that they were pale, quite ashen. His first thought was that it was the dog that had frightened them. Then he asked them what had caused their fear and why they were following him, for it all seemed "curiouser and curiouser," as Alice in Wonderland might have put it.

The man with the girl blinked, then asked Dennis who the person was that had been walking with him. Puzzled, Dennis replied that he was alone—no one had walked with him. The man insisted that the stranger who walked with Dennis was what had attracted them to follow him as he walked away from the barn. The person wasn't someone they knew, yet one who seemed uncannily different.

"What stranger? What person?" Dennis asked, suddenly becoming aware of the change that had taken place in him—the glow and flow of light and warmth seemed to have gone from him, though the feelings of love for these people remained. This sense of love lingered on and was to remain with him for some days afterwards.

"The man who was with you, walking with you, was here—and we saw him! But, when the dog's nose touched your hand, and as the dog turned and went back into the trees, the person with you just disappeared!"

Dennis began to tremble. Not only did he fail to understand what was happening to him, he had seen no-one with him or near him other than this very frightened couple who now stood staring at him. Yet he believed them. Instinctively, he knew they were too frightened *not* to be telling the truth. Then they described the man they had seen as tall and very distinct. He was clearly defined in the light, more so than Dennis had been. He had walked with Dennis, matching his stride if not also his thoughts. Then, when the dog came, he just disappeared! He simply vanished into thin air!

Leaving the couple, pale and shaken as they were, to go back into the barn, Dennis felt he had had enough. He made his way home to his farm, still full of the feelings of love.

He felt more strongly than ever that he had to talk to someone about the experience. The only one he could approach was the Rev Dr Louis Bosch, the Superintendent Methodist Minister who lived in Pietersburg. Even so, he hesitated about this, for he felt the Minister was too important to share this experience with and that he would probably laugh off the whole thing as some hallucination that comes to those who go to certain parties. So he decided not to tell the Minister and to wait and see what would happen. He would live with the experience and see whether this visitation that had come to him so mysteriously would also as mysteriously explain itself. This proved to be a very difficult choice, but with that choice Dennis was to live from the mid-eighties until November 2000 when, meeting the Rev Bosch in the Mall at Rosebank in Johannesburg by accident, he decided he had to tell him.

As Dennis told his experience, the Minister sensed some of the answers to the questions he had asked himself about the changes he had seen in Dennis while he was still in the Pietersburg-Potgietersrus area. Dennis had gone on to teach in the Sunday School; he had grown in an ever-deepening spirituality that was pregnant with an equally deepening sense of love for people; he had emanated a love for God and His Word and a strong desire to pursue his love and search for truth. It was clear, now, that Dennis's life had dramatically changed. It would never be the same again since the night of that party.

These days Dennis is involved with teaching individuals and groups what the Bible is all about, and what life is all about according to the Gospel and its truth. He experiences growth in mind and spirit he could never have thought possible, as well as an enthusiasm pertaining to the things of God. He has got no closer to an answer of what happened that night and who the stranger was that walked with him; neither has he any conception of what the dog had seen and done, and why. But he has been a different man ever since.

How do we, the readers of this experience, understand what happened? In the end, what does it say to us?

Rev Dr Louis Bosch
Yeoville
Gouteng
South Africa

RE-PROGRAMMED BY GOD!

Cornelia Raath

This is the story about an amazing young woman in Pretoria, South Africa, who had everything she could dream of—until a terrible accident wiped her memory—leaving her without the ability to count or remember anything from her past! The story is told by Cornelia Raath, a computer expert now re-programmed by God!

THERE WAS A TIME when I was amazingly successful in the world's eyes. In my first 26 years I conquered more challenges than many people could hope to achieve in a lifetime. No challenge was too much for me and my brilliant brain!

I completed my degree in Electronic Engineering—a difficult degree for many. Thereafter I worked day and night as an electronic engineer at the CSIR (Council for Scientific and Industrial Research in South Africa), completing the world's first computer programme on Neural Networks—the simulation of the human brain to make decisions, still used daily by Denel and the S.A. Air Force. At the same time I studied Computer Science part-time through the University of South Africa.

Over weekends I got my adrenaline rushing by doing parachuting with the Air Force, also engaging in white water rafting and bungee jumping at the Victoria Falls (at the time the highest natural bungee in the world). Other regular pastimes were motor-crossing with my bike and Kung-Fu. No challenge was too difficult for me, physical or mental!

But then my life changed dramatically.

One evening, after repairing a friend's computer, I was making my way to the gymnasium on my motorbike when right ahead of me a lady skipped a stop-street. I was thrown off the bike. My helmet came off and I hit the kerbstone with a sickening impact that crushed my skull. A man driving behind me had seen the whole thing! In his eyewitness report he stated that when he reached me lying on the road, I was blue in the face, not breathing, my eyes turned back.

Basically, I was dead! But the man lost no time in giving me the kiss of life, and I began to breathe again.

I had been on my way to gym and had no ID on me. So I was refused entry to two private hospitals. Consequently I was admitted to the hospital as unknown and brain-dead, and left to die!

It was only the next morning that I received surgery. Once again the eyewitness came to my rescue, insisting they attend to me. In the operation that followed I was treated for cracked skull and brain haemorrhage.

It was only after I woke up from a coma that lasted three weeks that my new life, as I now know it, began.

My father had died a month before the accident, yet I had no memory of him. It's as though I'd never known a father! All my knowledge and expertise from my university studies had vanished. All that I knew—and know—of my previous life is what I see in photographs, certificates, university articles and journals. I also had to learn to talk and learn to walk again. At the age of 28 I was medically boarded from my job—a job that had clearly given me total work satisfaction, judging from the fact that my ultimate holiday experience had apparently been to work throughout the night at the CSIR!

For about two and a half years I avoided people because of all my inabilities and losses. Imagine, not being able to count anymore! Please, dear readers, don't take the abilities you have for granted! Praise the Lord at every opportunity for every ability you have, however obvious and simple it may seem! Like counting, speaking, walking! Just to be able to speak again, to walk again, and to count, has made me so happy!

What brought about the change in me? I was surely touched by an angel! While attending the "Being Refreshed in the Holy Spirit" weekend, the Lord—or his angel—touched me at some time during the weekend. It was with a shock and great excitement that I suddenly realised, on the Sunday morning, that I had *ten* fingers - not the usual twenty I believed I had and had insisted I had since my accident. When confronted with this counting issue, I always believed I was the only person that could count in this world, based on having had a distinction in third-year maths at university! But the truth was I'd never been able to count since my accident more than four years ago.

Somewhere between being filled by the Holy Spirit, experiencing God's touch, and so may prayers said on my behalf, I regained my ability to count! Praise God for answered prayers—not in our time, but in his perfect time!

Certainly, I still have difficulty reading with comprehension, watching television with understanding, with concentration and, of course, there's the severe memory loss. But then I've found the Lord as my Saviour.

As a new Christian I was faced with the concept of forgiveness—forgiving a lady that was found guilty of reckless and negligent driving in two courts, but who still insists that I, as biker, was at the wrong place at the wrong time. In her eyes, she did nothing wrong. The ordeal resulted in me ending up in Denmar nursing home for a month, trying to work through my frustrations. Eventually I was able to send her a letter of forgiveness. Once I did this my life opened up—in spite of my occasional frustrations at my inability to commit anything to memory, or recall anything from memory; also, in spite of being permanently in pain.

People who knew me before the accident said they had the impression I considered my brain as my god! With my brain—and physical fitness, of course—I needed no one else to overcome all challenges. Then suddenly the mainstay on which I had depended—my brain!—was gone! Now there's a new dependence, for surely God wants me to rest my weight fully on him.

I've now come to realise it's not at all important what milestones, qualifications, status symbols or business successes I'm able to achieve in this life. The only important thing in this life is to have a living relationship with the Lord—to rest my weight fully on our heavenly Father. After all, the son of the living God has asked us who are heavy laden to bring our burdens to him, hasn't he?

I prayed for a piece of Scripture to sum up my testimony, but not having the ability to read books, articles or paragraphs on the subject with understanding, I didn't succeed -- at first. Then, while listening to "Impact Radio," a text was given that expressed the message of my story in a nutshell!—"What good is it for a man to gain the whole world, yet forfeit his soul?" (Mark 8: 36).

At the bottom of my Life Application Study Bible the following discussion is given on the verse:

Jesus said that a world centred on possessions, position, or power [in my case qualifications, worldly success and achievements] is ultimately worthless. Whatever you have on earth is only temporary—it cannot be exchanged for your soul. If you work hard at getting what you want, you might eventually have a pleasurable life, but in the end you will find it hollow and empty...

Are you willing to make the pursuit of God more important than the selfish pursuit of pleasure (and success)? Follow Jesus, and you will know what it means to live abundantly now and to have eternal life as well.

Whenever and wherever I am, my ever-present pain still blocks out many thoughts from my mind. It was the same thing a while ago during a recent Quiet Morning Counselling Course and Family Camp. I was unable to concentrate much on the message because of the ever-present, intense pain all over my body. But then God spoke to me and said I should inspire people to cope with pain rather than to focus so much on the pain itself.

"Okay, Lord—here I go!" I said. I was desperately talking to Mike, my minister, a while ago about being too disillusioned to go forward in prayer. Disillusionment, and depression, like negative thinking, prevents one from seeing healing where it's desperately needed. Mike really opened my eyes by his sympathetic reply—that I should always keep in mind that maybe, just *maybe*, complete healing is not in God's plan for me.

Nick Sailer, a Lay Preacher, spoke a while ago on healing, and it was while I was at home rewriting and going through my notes as well as his notes again and again that the Holy Spirit pointed this out to me: we can experience God's gift of healing in one or two ways: either the burden is removed or changed, or God changes us through his power of endurance. That is where our burden no longer causes us anguish, sorrow and pain. Instead, the miraculous God gives us the ability to endure and be victorious over our burden, and this makes us stronger and wiser in faith and brings us closer to him!

So, I'm also now learning to change my attitude towards my pains and aches. Rather than only complaining about it when asked how I'm doing, I now reply positively with: "Yes, I'm in pain, it's true, but the Lord's healing me!"

Finally, there's one particular verse in the Bible that *really* sustains me and keeps me going from moment to moment. It's Romans 8:18, where Paul says he considers that which we suffer in this present time to be insignificant compared to the glory that will be revealed to us—in other words, our current pain, our suffering, in this microscopic timespan of our present mutable and fleeting time on earth is nothing—nothing!—compared to the glory we'll experience in God's timeless eternity!

Cornelia Raath
Pretoria, South Africa

A LIFE'S WALK WITH ANGELS

Emelia Hardy

I'VE ALWAYS BELIEVED there are angels all around us.

I believe it was an angel that handed me to mama when I was born, for there is none other like her. What better way to start my life!

When I was a little girl daddy would beat me—but I think the angels held his hand back before he could hurt me real bad.

When I was put into the convent I believed the angels picked up the hand of the little girl that lay in the bed next to mine and put her hand into mine when I was crying to comfort me, to let me know I wasn't alone. I believe it was an angel that put me into the hands of the sweetest nun that ever was—the only sweet nun that was there.

As I grew a little older I believe it was an angel that brought me to the right door in the middle of the night to find my mama after not seeing her for almost two years.

When I was fifteen I believe it was angel that made the bleeding stop after I had stabbed myself in the wrist because I didn't want to live anymore. I couldn't face life after being raped and left pregnant.

I believe it was an angel that led me to find a jar of peanut butter and a package of Kool-Aid in order to feed my baby and myself for two days because my alcoholic husband never came home with any formula or food. He just never came home from partying.

I believe it was an angel that kept me alive after each beating I received from my first husband. It was so sad that he beat me to the extent that on two different occasions I miscarried my babies. I believe it was the angels of God that brought my babies to heaven and who are taking care of them now.

After finally escaping from the abuse of my husband with a divorce, I believe it was an angel that made me look up at work to find someone looking at me with soft brown eyes, someone that turned out to be the love of my life.

I believe it was an angel that came into the house in the middle of the night to turn me over onto my back where I lay unconscious as a result of a gas leak—the gas leak that killed the love of my life who lay dying next to me. The doctors said that if I hadn't been on my back I would have died too. I was on my stomach to begin with and I truly believe that God's angel came into the house and rolled me over onto my back, because gas is heavy and stays real close to the floor, and my being on my back meant that my face was a head's width away from being in direct contact with the gas.

I must have not paid attention to my angel's warnings when I married again years later to a man that I should have stayed away from—a man that thought nothing of breaking our sacred vows to one another.

With my life the way it was with my second marriage, I was always tied up in knots inside. I received phone calls from different girls that he was seeing; of course, he denied that he was seeing any of them. You see, I was married to a womaniser—so I know first-hand what a womaniser acts like.

My husband was never home. He preferred to be at the bars at night, drinking, playing darts and pool with his friends, then having his friends cover for him when he went out back of the club and had sex with his girlfriends. (Not all at once—different ones for different nights.) He even had one of his girlfriends meet him on the job sights (he was and still is in the construction business); she would go to the job, bring a blanket with a lunch and head for the woods with him where more than one appetite was taken care of.

He never had too much love left in him by the time he got home.

I waited up all hours of the night for him to come home, crying my heart out, asking God to bring him home to me and to his children.

I believe that it was an angel that sent a friend of mine to me with a book to read. It was a Christian Handbook. I started to read it one night while waiting for my husband to come home. I was still reading it when he managed to get himself through the door and up to the bedroom, drunk, hardly able to walk—yet he had driven his van home. I took the book that I had in my hands, which I had read more than half way, and flung it across the sofa where I was sitting. "What good will this do?" I asked myself.

I was becoming angry with GOD! "Why?" I asked him, "Why is there no peace in this world for me? Will I ever be happy? Will you ever answer any of my prayers? Don't you even hear me?!"

I went to bed hurt and in despair.

I believe a few days later that it was an angel straight from God that took that very same book and put it back into my hands when I found myself in my usual dilemma of waiting for my husband to come home.

This time I read with great interest! My eyes were drawn to a diagram of a circle in the book with Jesus at the top of it. I read all about giving myself to Jesus—of how He can help us. There was a sinner's prayer at the end of the book. It said if you read it twice then you really meant it!

I fell to my knees and I said the prayer for the second time. I held the book up to the ceiling and cried out: "Help me, Lord! Help me!" I almost screamed as I cried out. The tears were burning my eyes.

The next thing I knew I woke up on the floor with the book still in my hands. And I was totally at peace! I asked myself, did this really happen?

Oh God, did it happen? I felt different. I was floating on air. I asked again, "Help me God. Show me that this really happened—that I didn't just dream it?"

I walked outside into the yard looking to see if my husband's van was there, thinking that he might have come home while I was sleeping on the floor in the living room. But he hadn't. It was now 2 a.m. The pain in my heart started to settle in once more—but at that moment I saw shooting lights and it looked like it was coming from the sky!

I ran around to the front of the house and I saw the most beautiful sight that I had ever seen in my life! It took my breath away! Yes, yes—it was an aurora! An aurora with many colours! "Oh God," I yelled, "It's beautiful!" Then I noticed that all of this was taking place right over the Church!

I knelt down on the ground and thanked God for showing me such a wonderful thing! It was as if all the angels in heaven were dancing in the sky with bright beautiful colours right above the Church! It was the answer I was looking for.

I'll never forget it!

Another year went by. My husband only got worse, but I got stronger, for I was a Christian now. I had accepted The Lord.

Nevertheless I tried everything humanly possible to try and get things to change with my husband but failed. I finally decided I had to leave. I couldn't take the other women any longer. I prayed and prayed that God wouldn't be angry with me for giving up.

Again I found myself waiting up for my husband to come home. I sat on the outside step praying to God, asking Him to forgive me. I remember saying out loud at 1:30 a.m.: "Please God, please let this be okay."

And again I saw lights shooting in the sky!

I ran around the house to get a better look—and there it was again! Another aurora! And again, with all the colours dancing across the sky! And, as before, right over the Church! All I could think of was that my angels were back to console me. It was almost as though they were saying, "It's okay, Emelia. Everything will be okay!" Again I dropped to my knees and thanked God for the beautiful colours in the sky—and I waved to the angels as they danced by!

I'll never forget it!

* * *

My brother Jerry, who was a servant of God, had a brain tumour and no one knew about it. I was in a restaurant with him and noticed something was wrong. I walked him out of the building and he became very unsteady on his feet. He was much bigger than I was and I could no longer hold him up. But I could feel the angels all around us. They held him up so I was able to wrap my arms around him and whisper the Lord's Prayer in his ear. The angels continued to hold him until help arrived. Their presence was unbelievable!

When Jerry was undergoing chemotherapy he became very sick at the dinner table one night. He threw up all over the table, floors, and cupboards. Once again the angels were there, pinching my nose so I couldn't smell anything because they knew I would get just as sick smelling it. Not only did they keep me from smelling it, they gave me enough time to clean up the mess.

I put Jerry in God's hands. One day, while changing my bed, I began to cry and couldn't stop. I loved my brother so much. I didn't want him to die. I was crying so loud. My head was pounding, my nose ran, my eyes burned from all the tears. Then the angle of God touched me.

"Why are you crying?" the voice asked. "I thought you put Jerry in God's hands?"

I stopped crying at once and rose from the bed. I looked into the mirror. There were no signs that I had been crying. I didn't even have to blow my nose! A peace fell over me. I knew at that moment that Jerry would die, but that there would be a time that I would be able to talk to him one more time and that God would let me know when that time came.

The whole family went to visit for Thanksgiving Day dinner. Jerry was so sweet but he didn't know anyone. His tumour was in his brain. Before he became so ill he had told me a story. He said, "Sis, don't be sad for me. I want you to be happy." How could I be happy when my brother, who was only thirty-nine, was dying! He said, "I prayed for this, sis. I wasn't being the person that I should have been. I slid away from God and I wanted to come back to where I was before, so I prayed to God that he would bring me back. I also told Him that it didn't matter how He did it. 'No matter what it takes Lord, bring me back'—and Praise God, He brought me back! And sis, He's taking me home to be with Him!"

Jerry was so excited when he told me that story! I was happy for him and sad for myself.

I went to visit him during my summer vacation. Jerry was in so much pain in his head. I couldn't stand to see it any more. I got down on my knees and asked God to give me the overflow of his pain—and God did! Jerry seemed a little better. I heard him tell his wife that the pain wasn't as bad as before. 'Praise God!' I thought to myself.

When it was time to leave and return home Jerry came up to the window of my car and told me how he hated to see me leave. I told him I was sorry but I had to get back home.

"You don't understand, sis," he said. "I really hate to see you leave"

"I really hate to leave, Jerry, but I have to get back to work."

"You still don't understand," he smiled, and he reached in the window to give me a kiss. Then he whispered in my ear: "You have to be careful what you pray for. How's your headache?"

His words took my breath away. There was no one in the room when I knelt down to pray for the overflow of his pain. How could Jerry know what I asked the Lord?

Then I realised that God's angels must have been there with me. I thought about it for a minute and remembered the warmth and peace that I felt just before Jerry's pain came into my head.

It was surely one of God's angels that whispered into Jerry's ear and told him what I had done, for it was only God's angels that heard me.

My brother got progressively worse as time went by, but he went on for almost three more years.

Then one day, when I stopped off to see mama for a minute, I flew back up out of my chair.

"What's the matter?" she asked, alarmed.

I believe it was an angel that pulled me right back out of that chair. An angel of God had touched me!

"I have to go home right now," I said.

"Why?" she asked.

"I have to go call Jerry. It's time, mama, it's time."

"Oh Emelia," mama replied, "Don't do this to yourself. You know he hasn't been able to talk for ages. And he doesn't know who he is anymore."

Mama tried to talk me out of it but there was no way that anyone was going to convince me I wasn't going to be able to talk to Jerry. After all, it was a promise from God and one of His holy angels had just touched me. I had waited three years for this and I wasn't going to ignore it.

Sure enough, when I called, it was Jerry himself who answered the phone, and he was as lucid as ever! I talked to him for over a better part of two hours. I should say that he did most of the talking. When we were done Jerry told me that he would be going home soon, but I already knew that. I also knew that would be the last time I would ever talk to him again.

Three weeks later I lifted the phone to call Jerry at the hospital, but I hung up the phone before the call went through. I hung up because I knew that at that second my Jerry had died. I could feel the angel's arms around me, holding me up the way they had held Jerry up three years before. I could feel the peace flowing from them to me. It was a feeling I will never forget!

Oh yes, I believe there are angels all around us.

Emelia Hardy[2]
Dover, New Hampshire, USA

---

[2] **Note**: Emelia Hardy's full story is told in her book *Why Daddy, Why*, published by iUniverse Inc, 2002.

89

FULL CIRCLE TO GOD

Albert J. Dion

WHAT I'M ABOUT TO WRITE ABOUT took place in the mid-eighties. At that time I was living in Winston-Salem, North Carolina, and had been there for sixteen years. (I'm told this is part of the Bible belt.)

I had given myself to the Creator at the age of eighteen. I knew nothing of what to expect of my new life and it wasn't long before I was stumbling in the dark, for my seed didn't make it to good soil. My heart rejoices in the knowledge that we have a wonderful God that looks upon us with love. His lessons are always for our own good, and if they involve suffering, he will use it to bring us into full maturity; so, in a sense, we sometimes suffer to come full circle. All things in life are to build faith and spiritual character. Sowing is important, but reaping allows our potential to come to full circle.

Remember always to hold all that God had taught you to be true. None of his lessons are to be taken lightly. Keep them close in the true place of your being, the centre of your heart, and always know that God and His ways are good for your every need.

Three years after accepting Christ as my Lord and Savoir, I was already in a downhill battle. The road I travelled was of my own doing. The Creator had His way, so, like a loving father, He allowed me to experience life as I chose. Even the mother and father I was given in this life, after teaching me all they could to give me a good strong background, would let me make my own decisions when I reached my manhood. They never told me how to think, how to act, what I should or shouldn't do. Consequently I would look back on the things I was taught and admit to them that I was wrong and they were right. And yet neither one of them would say, "I told you so." I love my parents very much and they always loved me—even with my mistakes.

Our heavenly father manifests much, much more patience and understanding than our earthly parents, as you will see from the story you're about to read concerning the event that took place when I was twenty-one years of age. I only had a vague notion of what was going on in my life at that time. I knew something was wrong and I needed help. I still wasn't fully aware of God's love, that same love that could have delivered me from myself.

The lessons that come from the virtue of God are building blocks for the heritage of who we become. The Creator has been very good to me, both in the good times and the bad times alike. He allows the bad times into our lives in order for us to learn. The Creator has control over both good and bad. Even though we are free to choose which road to travel, He uses the road we take to bring us to a better place, so all is true and useful for His purpose for us.

The event in my life that illustrates this took place on a Sunday. My wife and I attended church, and, in fact, I was doing some work at the Baptist Ministry. It's a day we will never forget!

We got home before the afternoon ended and my wife went to prepare something to eat and I thought I'd relax in the living room. All of a sudden I wasn't feeling too well and decided to lie down on the sofa. I had already taken my shirt off. I was feeling feverish, so I went and got a wet washcloth to wipe my face and chest down. I felt so strange—it was hard to focus. I looked around the room and couldn't make any sense of anything! I was burning up. I continued to use the washcloth on my face and chest in order to cool down, but it wasn't working so I turned on the air conditioner. My whole body was feeling sick from top to bottom. My mid-section felt like I wanted to vomit. I had no idea that this was going to get even worse! It was getting harder for me to think, or, indeed, to focus on any one thought. I made my way to the bathroom and was violently sick! I imagined this ought to make me feel better—but I was wrong. My wife came to see what ailed me; she was scared and didn't have any idea what to do for me.

Whatever had gripped me pulled me down even deeper; for I now lost any kind of rational awareness. I had very little control of my thoughts. The wonder of it is that I'm able to remember it in such detail!

I tried to get away from myself. I walked into the kitchen, then the bedroom, and then to every room in the house—but I still couldn't escape from whatever had possessed me! I did this over and over again, many times, and still I was not able to talk to my wife. My thoughts were a whirl of confusion and I was unable to put anything in its proper place. As I was going around from room to room, my thinking was doing the same. I knew something was very wrong! Once more I managed to make my way to the bathroom where I was sick again, then walked back into the living room where I collapsed on the floor. I was in a cold sweat, yet on fire. The feeling in my chest was like a three-inch rubber band squeezing inward while the inside of my chest was pushing outward. I was really frightened! I wasn't allowed any solace, no easement. I was in trouble and had no idea what needed to be done. I couldn't get up from all fours. I sank even deeper when I tried to fight back. At that moment in my life I had no hope, peace, or joy. I was not content—I had no vestige of a happy spirit that dwelled inside me. My perspective of God's presence or blessings in my life had diminished to nothing. And yet I preserved a dim awareness that I hadn't asked my heavenly father to render help where it was needed. I thought I could handle it. This, then, was the cul-de-sac, or the impasse, that I had reached as a result of doing things my way! The result was chaos.

As I said, the thinking part of me was not able to focus on anything. The speaking part was not able to converse with my wife. My mind wasn't my own. I was feeling very strange, as if a fiery dart had pierced my very being. Was I heading for a stroke? Or a heart attack? Or losing grip on my mental faculties? It was a nightmare in reality! I felt like I was being held hostage with no way back to who I was. I realised that even with all my strength I was not able to do anything to get out from where I was. I still had no idea what needed to be done. I had a real sickening feeling in my insides, wanting this to end! With still no control over my thoughts, my concentration was lost. I was confused. I couldn't even think!

I finally managed to get myself on my feet and on my way once again to the bathroom where I could take some kind of refuge from whatever had taken me over. When I passed the mirror I got to see myself for the first time— something I never want to see again! I just stood there staring at myself. It was not me, yet I knew it was. My entire face stared back at me, haggard and deformed. It was frightful! It took my breath away and I fainted within myself. I was so desperate for this to end. I still had no idea why or how I came to be under attack, helpless in the path of the fiery darts from what I now call 'The Instigator,' or 'The Aggravator,' also known to me as 'The Agitator.'

I'm not certain how long it took this nightmare to come full circle, but I'd have to say it was the better part of two hours. I know that God didn't do this to me; nevertheless, as I said, God does allow things to come into our lives for spiritual growth. God can't be tempted, nor will he tempt any man. So it would be safe to say that what happened during this time span was not of His doing, but that He used the nightmarish experience to bring about good—for what took place next was far from anything I had, or have, ever experienced in my life. Still, not knowing what was happening to me, I was still not calling on the only one that could rescue and restore me.

I came out of the bathroom with a feeling of hopelessness and was desperate to find answers. I went back into the living room and sat on the sofa, a picture window behind me and a wall in front of me separating the kitchen and living room. My understanding was still not intact. Negative thoughts consumed me. I felt overwhelmed by a sense of hopelessness within me and around me—there was no room for good. I sat there, completely exhausted. My body couldn't take much more, my mind going in a confusion of different directions. I stared at the wall in front of me—and then it happened!

Something came *through* the wall. It had no form. I can only describe what was before me as a very strong, hideous and authoritative evil spirit! I was completely overwhelmed by its presence. I was filled with terror as it moved slowly towards me. My wife had entered the room, but she could see nothing, near to panic in her concern for me.

I didn't know if I was being pulled into the world of this evil or if evil had come to me!

I was suddenly tuned into this mass that was in front of me. I realised now just how weak our minds, spirits and souls really are. The only way I was going to be able to get out of this would be with God!

It's difficult to put down on paper the intense feelings of emotions that flowed through me; also, to write about the place where the true one sits. As we know, we shouldn't allow feelings to interfere with faith. I know without a doubt that it was Christ who pulled me through.

It was a very overpowering, frightful feeling! I sat up on the edge of the sofa, gripped by this strong fear. To describe it as best as I can, I would have to say my feelings were of complete helplessness—a sense of self-loathing, intense hate, overwhelming negativity. My mind was losing the battle, feeling sick from top to bottom and completely disoriented. Then I did what I should have done right from the beginning! I asked God to come! I told Him I was nothing without Him! This force was too strong. I was no match for it.

The Heavenly Creator gave me something I had lost sight of. I somehow asked the spirit of supplication to please allow the spirit to do my bidding. It was strange—things began to slow down. I had been in another time, not the human 'clock time' but another time. Yet I was still sitting on the edge of the sofa. As this mass was moving towards me I stood up with my head bent over, looking at this thing with no form yet filled with pure hatred. I screamed as loud as I could at it: "No, you can't have me!"

The evil force was gone! I came to all my senses. I was no longer confused or incoherent. I fell back onto the sofa. I was completely restored with movement. My head pain was gone and my stomach was no longer sick. My chest no longer had pain. It had finally ended.

I still sit and think about what happened to me that day. Anyone reading this can never imagine the intensity, or the reality, of what I saw and felt. It's hard to write about something about the bad or good spirit, even though both are on a different plateau—different, and always at war with each other. Indeed, I'm a perfect example of that battle. I'll never forget it!

I realised years later that this fiery dart I experienced was for a purpose. It was God allowing evil to approach me in order that something good might come out of the experience.

I worked for R.J. Reynolds at the time this happened to me and I started doing a lot of studying of the Bible. I had God's word with me at all times—at work, during doctor appointments, anywhere where I might have the opportunity to read. I would go nowhere without my little Bible.

After some time had passed I was getting into the meat of the word of God. Yet I can remember being warned not to study anything other than the sincere milk of God's word. Many times I was touched by the Holy Spirit with a sense of what I was doing was not good. So on these occasions I would pray about it.

I continued to press on with my life thinking that I was doing well, that I had good principles; but then, while reading the Bible during one of my breaks at work, I heard a voice—and it called my name. I turned around to see, thinking it was one of the guys I worked with, but no one was there. I heard my name again. It was deep within me, and then I realised it was from God. My angel said to me, "Your faith is not strong enough to sustain." I replied, "I'm reading and it's all having an effect on me."

So once again I didn't listen. I was not surrendering to God but trying to take control. I was headstrong, and that was something God clearly disapproved of. I had more strength in me than I had had in my whole life, yes—but I kept going in the direction I thought was right and in my own strength. Because I still didn't listen fully to what my angel had said to me, I was still caught up in the circle. Nevertheless I *did* continue to feast and get drunk on the word of God and I'm a better person for it. Praise the Lord that He has it all under control.

I'm glad He allowed this strange thing to take place with me at my home on that Sunday afternoon. I thought I was strong, but I was shown otherwise. I'm no match for the evil one. I'm glad my Heavenly Father cared enough and had time to show me just how weak I really am. The answer? Let go—and let God! Only then can one grow and come full circle—to God.

Bend us, O Lord, where we are hard and cold,
in your refiner's fire come purify the gold
Though suffering comes, and evil crouches near,
still our Living God is reigning, he is reigning here.

G. Kendrick / C. Rolinson,
Kingsway's Thank you Music/altered

Albert J. Dion
Concord, NH, USA

PRAYER CHANGES THINGS

Allison Hislop

FOR OVER THIRTY YEARS I have had a fear of cancer since my Mum died in 1970 from the disease, leaving two sisters and myself. Every lump and bump sent me running to the doctor in total panic. In August 2001 I was diagnosed with ovarian cancer. This came completely out of the blue, for although I had felt unwell for some time I put it down to my age. (I am fifty-one years old.) I was admitted to hospital on Monday 15th August and then began a series of tests. On the 14thAugust I asked the Lord to give me a verse I could hold on to. As I was reading through the psalms my eyes paused at Psalm 77, particularly verse 14: "You are the God who performs miracles." On the 18thAugust, the night after I had had my operation, I was reading through the Psalms again and asking the Lord for a verse that I might cling to. I read Psalm 71. I had finished reading the Psalm before I realised what I had read. Verse 20 leaped out at me and I thought this *had* to be the Lord speaking to me: "Though you have made me see troubles, many and bitter, you will restore my life again; from the depths of the earth you will again bring me up."

I could not believe what was happening to me. I was in total shock, especially when I was told it was cancer. One of my ovaries had stuck to the bowel, so part of my bowel had to be removed. I immediately asked the Lord to stay close by my side, as I did not understand what was happening. As the days progressed I told the Lord that if He raised me up I would serve Him in whatever way He wanted. I asked Him to allow me to see my young son, who is 11 years old, grow up—and would He allow me to see my husband become a Christian?

I was able to testify in hospital and share the verses that the Lord had given me with staff that did not always understand.

I came home to recuperate and two weeks after the operation began to be sick. I was taken back into hospital and lay there for about ten days. During this time I was taken up to the Western Hospital in Edinburgh and saw the oncologist who talked to me about my forthcoming chemotherapy. The Doctor said he wanted me admitted to the Western straightaway. I lay in the Western for another two weeks as I had contracted an infection, so I was being pumped full of antibiotics. I was told I was a very sick lady but nevertheless a very fit lady. Still, I could not eat, as I was continually being sick. An obstruction was ruled out but I appeared to be getting weaker by the minute. I knew people were praying for me. My own church held prayer meetings and I received many cards and letters full of encouragement. Family and friends, too, were constantly praying and I know prayers were prayed in America, Australia and Budapest. One friend said she knew the Lord would heal me and gave me Scriptures that the Lord had given her (1 Peter: 4:19 & 1 Peter 5:10). I eventually stopped being sick and was allowed home. Before I came home I had one dose of chemo to start me off so to speak.

Unfortunately, ten days later I began to be sick again and was re-admitted to the Western. The doctors were talking about a blockage and another operation. After two days I began to feel better and suddenly my sickness stopped. I asked to go home and although one doctor said I was twisting his arm, I was allowed to go.

I did not look back after this and, although I was very weak to the extent I could not walk far and had to use a wheelchair, I began to eat small amounts. Being on a low residue diet, I was only allowed certain foods. Nevertheless I continued to eat and was not sick.

I felt as though I had reached the bottom and remembered Psalm 71 and how the Lord would raise me up from the depths of the earth. I was certainly in the depths now. I could go no further.

I began my chemotherapy, which was to be six sessions comprising of two types of chemo, one quite light and one very harsh. The chemo was given at three weekly intervals and took five and a half hours to administer. I was told I would suffer hair loss, fatigue, tingling, loss of feeling in my fingers and toes and joint pain. I can say that apart from the hair loss and slight joint pain, which lasted for three days, I did not really suffer any other symptoms. This was because of prayer. There was no other explanation. PRAYER CHANGES THINGS.

The Deacons from my church came to anoint me and pray over me (James 5:13-16). This was a very special time and I felt so much at peace.

The chemo continued, my lovely blonde hair fell out and my targets (the blood count which signifies cancer cells) fell rapidly from 3500 (1st session) to 15 (untraceable—4th session). I began to put weight on, grow stronger and feel well. The doctors and nurses could not believe how I was reacting to the treatment.

I was told I would need to undergo a hysterectomy on February 20th, after the chemo had finished in January. I was not particularly looking forward to another operation but knew I would need it. On Wednesday February 15th I was due to see the oncologist. While driving up to Edinburgh I began to think of some words I had either heard or read about the Sun of Righteousness and healing. I could not get these words out of my mind and later asked my step-mum if she knew where they came from. She looked up her concordance and quoted Malachi 4:2: "But for you who revere my name, the Sun of Righteousness will rise with healing in His wings." I praised God for this word. The next day we were due to visit friends in Lancashire and on our return I found a card waiting. It was from a friend in the church. In it she had asked the Lord to give her a verse for me. She quoted Malachi 4:2 and also Psalm 30:1-3, 11 &12. I was very excited.

The following Monday (February 18th) my husband, Matthew and I were driving towards Berwick-upon-Tweed about 7.50 in the morning. Matthew was due to visit his new school, which he will start in September, God willing. We drove along the main road, up the hill beside the local golf course and I asked John what the bright light in the sky was. He said it was the sun. As we came to the top of the hill, I could the sun in all its brilliance. It was so bright we could hardly see the road and I knew straightaway without any doubt that this was the Sun of Righteousness. The sun did not leave us all the way to Berwick, or on our return. The clouds did not cover it once. We lost the brightness due to the road dipping and turning but the sun remained in the sky, totally brilliant. I was stunned and very excited. *Praise the Lord!*

I was due in hospital the next day with my operation the following day. I experienced such peace as I repeated the verse from Malachi over and over again.

Early on Thursday morning (February 21st) I read these words from *God Calling*, a little book I have owned for many years: "Nothing can hurt. The way is plain. You do not need to see far ahead. Just one step at a time with Me. The same light to guide you as the Hosts of Heaven know—the Sun of Righteousness Himself."

The surgeon came to tell me the result of my operation and he said, "Good news, there was no cancer found!" Praise God from whom all blessings flow. This was not coincidence but God-incidence! Later on another doctor told me that I would have 5—10 years, but as I said to the oncologist later, the God who formed me in my mother's womb will decide when He takes me.

The following week I saw the oncologist who hugged me and said I was 99.9% clear and after a thorough search one or two cells were found. I was to have three light chemos to make sure all cancer cells were dealt with. The church held a Prayer and Praise night and what a wonderful occasion that was. To give God all the glory and thanks is just wonderful.

I have my moments and on one occasion was feeling quite low when my daily reading was from John 15—the vine and the branches. Verse 3 leaped out at me: "You are already clean because of the word I have spoken." What was the word? The Sun of Righteousness will rise with healing in His wings.

Since then I have gone from strength to strength and now my hair is growing back and I have put weight on. I have just had a check-up and was told I was symptom-free and disease free.

How do I sum up what has happened? I will never be the same person again. The Lord has changed me totally and I find it a privilege to tell others of what God is doing and has done in my life. Do I get frightened? Of course I do, especially when I'm due a check-up. I don't want to die at the moment—I told the Lord I have too much living to do. We live in dark and desperate days and I need to tell others of a loving Saviour who died for each one of us. Does Satan tempt? All the time and I know I am in the middle of a battle. He causes me to have odd pains, which naturally make me think dark thoughts—but I know I need to put on the whole armour and stand firm. (Eph: 6:10-18)

I know I have been healed but I need to trust the Saviour, not just every day but every moment of every hour. I still have so much to learn. I had the privilege of being elected a Deacon in our church recently and know this is another way of serving the Lord. I have spoken at a conference and also to many non-Christians bout the Lord. Many do not understand but I am only to sow the seed. The Lord will do the rest.

My prayer is that anyone who reads this testimony will be challenged to put their trust in a loving God and come to know Him as Saviour and Lord. Let me say to you, "God is faithful!" He has promised He will not give us more than we can bear, and through every trial He is always there for us.

Keep trusting, keep loving and keep your eyes firmly fixed on Jesus.

Loneliness

In a hospital
along a corridor
In a crowded ward
There lies a woman, quite still.

She gets lots of visitors
and an awful lot of flowers
The doctor comments that
she could start a florists.

I know she's getting well
She's coming home soon
Her treatment's going well
this has been such a boom.

As the weeks tick by
she becomes stronger and stronger
I ponder waiting for her to come home
I don't want her in hospital any longer.

Matthew J. Hislop (age 11)

I MET MY ANGEL FACE TO FACE...

Irene Letourneau

I AM A PERSON that finds great pleasure in making puzzles. Then I often ask myself why is it that I just enjoy making puzzles about angels? I made one called "An Angels Gift" and another one named "The American Angel." Are these little angels the Lord's gift to the people here on earth?

A time came when I had to leave my first husband after eighteen years of marriage. I asked the Lord to please watch over my children until I could get a place of my own to live and then go get my children to come and live with me.

Every night when I would try and go to sleep a calm peace would come over me right after I was done praying for my children—such a peace that it made me feel as though I was being told that the children would be okay. It took a while but then, one day, very early in the morning my little girl was knocking at my door with her sister and two little brothers waiting outside on the sidewalk because they had no idea which place was my apartment—but in my heart I knew it was an angel that took my little girl's hand and led her right to me! I went to bed that night thanking the Lord for sending His precious angel to help.

Now I only had one more of my children to fetch and that was my oldest son Jerry. After a while I was able to get him back, too. It was right after school was out for the summer. Now I had my family back. But later on down the road, my oldest son became very ill. A brain tumour, they said.

Oh my God! A brain tumour!

Yes, the day came when I had to bury my son. What a wonderful man he had turned out to be—a man that served the Lord! But, of course, it was Jerry's time to be taken home to Heaven. I never question the will of God but it didn't make it any easier to be looking down at him in his coffin. I really thank God for sending me His angels that day! I never would have gotten through it without their help.

When we think of angels we have a tendency to say that they are little girls. Well, I do believe that they come in all sizes and genders: Little boys, little girls, women, and the wonderful angel that God sent to me to be a father to my children whom they adore and a precious husband to me. After being alone for two years trying my best to raise my five children, what a welcoming angel to become the love of my life and still is after forty years!

What gets me to the point of being able to write this is what happened to me at the grocery store. My husband is now suffering from cancer, and he and I both being retired, the money is stretched to its limit. Having to buy groceries for the month and added medical supplies, I had no idea how we were going to make it through the month. I kept looking at the items that my husband was adding to the cart and wondered how in the world we were going to pay for it. I didn't want to worry him. I was walking down the isle pushing my cart trying to decide what items I could do without while my husband went to get a package of tomatoes, when and all of a sudden a woman walked up to me and said, "Hello, I am a Christian." I said to her, "That is so nice to hear. I'm glad to say that I am one too." Then she took my hand and opened it and put something into it, saying, "I want you to have this. Please take it and I thank you." Then off she went.

I opened my hand and was speechless! What she had put into my hand was a one hundred dollar bill! I quickly turned around and she was gone! When my husband came back to me with his tomatoes, I was crying! He asked me what was wrong and I told him what had just happened. We spent the next twenty minutes walking around the store trying to find her but never did. I completely fell apart because I had been praying the whole time I was in the store as to how I was going to be able to pay for everything!

She was a beautiful woman with black shoulder length hair and sparkling eyes. I will never forget the kind expression that was on her face. Truly, an angel sent from God.

I told different people about this. Then, coming out of Church one Sunday, I spoke to the pastor and his answer to me was, "The Lord's Angels work in mysterious ways." But I didn't need for him to tell me that, for I had years of experiencing it!

Now, after you have read this, do you think I believe in angels? Oh my Lord God in Heaven! I surely do! And I thank the Lord for having sent me that elegant angel. For in my heart I feel like this has been the angel that always made me feel like my children were okay.

To this day I still ask the Lord to continue to send His angels to keep watch over my children, and I just know in my heart and soul that He will! Just like I know that He is looking after my son Jerry.

And I know He will continue to bless us with His Angels! After all, I believe I came face to face with mine!

Irene Letourneau
Rochester, NH, USA

GOD'S GUINEA PIG

Rev. Margaret Freeman

WHILE WORKING OVERTIME one evening the phone rang rather persistently and, after some hesitation, I answered it. It was my father to say he had just got home from work to find a letter asking whether I could go into Guys immediately. It was already about 7.00pm so, if I was to go in that day, there was no time for me to go home. My mother and Sheila were both away, so I agreed with Dad that he would ring the hospital to say I was on my way. I asked him to pack up my night things and a few bits and pieces, collect me from work and take me in. I then bustled round to leave everything in the office as organised as possible, and left a letter to my boss on my desk saying "Goodbye". Then began five weeks of tests. I had catheters pushed up the veins of my arms and legs into and through my heart. I also had dye injected through my body under X-ray. At one time my arms had been so cut about that they both had to be splinted, and I had to sit by a bedridden patient for her to feed me my dinner. There were two younger girls on the ward having similar tests. It was 1948, the year of the great polio outbreak, and there were two "iron lungs" on the ward that rumbled day and night, and in a kind of conservatory built on the side of the ward were three TB patients. In a bed at the end of the ward was Pat, the hospital almoner, who herself had caught Polio. She'd been for a few days in a "lung", but had recovered apart from her legs. In a vain hope to get these working again they needed to be put in a swing over her bed every few hours and swung. I tried to help her and the busy nurses by swinging her legs. It was a hopeless task and she got very depressed. Trying to keep her going stopped me worrying about myself.

One morning we were being woken on the ward with a cup of tea when Pat called across the ward, "It's a boy!" She had her earphones on to listen to the 6.00am news. Princess Elizabeth had had a son, and we all drank the health of the new prince in rather tepid hospital tea.

At the end of the five weeks the physician, under whose care I was put while having the tests in this medical ward, came in, pulled the curtains round the bed, and sat down. This was it! Very gently and kindly he told me that my heart was far too damaged to survive such an untried operation and I could go home the next day. I was completely devastated. For a few moments my faith was gone, and thoughts of jumping out of the bathroom window raced through my brain. As I rushed past Pat's bed in the direction of the bathroom she called me back and asked me what Dr. Baker had said. Talking to her helped me to see things in perspective. I was ready to live for as long as God willed it and to die when he decided it was time. Also, my friend Will Power returned. Pat was also feeling depressed about her future and we cried together, but I went to bed quite calm and looking forward to going home next day.

Early next morning Sir Russell Brock came to see me. "Well, old thing," he said, "I've decided you would be a very good candidate for my new operation. You have, I think, about 75% chance of surviving the operation and about 50% of being better. Do you want to take the chance?" One thing about Sir Russell, he never beat about the bush! My first thought was of about the other 25% if there was no improvement and I was still alive. This was worrying. I asked him what could happen then. It seems I could be not very different or I could have brain damage or be paralysed. I had no doubt that I wanted the operation, and the rest was up to God. He then said that as I was going down so quickly the sooner the better and he would operate in ten days. Did I want to stay in hospital or go home for a week? As my parents were coming to get me that day in any case, I decided to go home. I have wondered many times why the two doctors did not get their act together before talking to me. The extremes of emotions I suffered in those two days were quite unnecessary, but I suppose it would have been worse if my hopes had been first raised and then dashed. I think there was a feeling among the doctors that some of the heart surgeons were looking for human guinea pigs, which in a sense they were, but in most of our cases our lives were over anyway. As far as I was concerned, I believed that God was telling me to trust him and not to put so much faith in my Will Power. He was making me submissive and humble.

It was quite a week. First I got a sniffle and my good intentions of doing my Christmas shopping had to be aborted while I stayed in and nursed my cold. I wrote my cards, putting in a covering note to say goodbye to my friends in case I didn't survive. Quite a few visitors came to see me and I realised I was going to be in hospital for Ines' Baptism and Confirmation. Sod's law!!

The following Monday I returned, this time to the surgical ward, for the operation on Thursday. There were two ops a week, one on a Monday and one on a Thursday. Each one would take about nine hours. As I was being admitted, the Monday patient returned from the theatre and was put in the plastic tent. She was alive, at least. Doris and I later became great friends. She had a Blalock operation and later was to become the first person to have a baby after heart surgery. Although still in the tent, Doris was so much better the next day that it gave me real hope. I learned that the other patients in the ward all got very anxious every time a heart patient went to theatre. As the nine hours went by, the ward would become very quiet. If the patient was not going to come back, sister would announce it to the ward at suppertime and the quiet would remain all evening. One evening sister brought me a letter from Pat, still in the medical ward, wishing me well.

On Tuesday the chaplain came to see me. Special prayers were being said for me in Southwark Cathedral and in the hospital chapel. He said he would come back that evening after the ward was quiet to hear my Confession and would bring me Communion early on Wednesday morning. Then on Wednesday evening after the nurses had got me all ready for the op., which was to start at 6.00am on Thursday, he would come and anoint me and give me last rites in case I did not come back. He was quite wonderful and popped in several times a day, sometimes just to see my visitors or to encourage the nurses, and I realise now what a difficult job he had, and how well he did it.

My parents never wavered in their support for me, but I think they may have talked over their fears with our family doctor who had become quite a friend.

All I know is that on the Wednesday evening, when I had said goodbye to my parents and had been bathed and dressed in a sterile gown and prepared for the operation, and was quietly waiting for the last visit from the Chaplain, my GP arrived, sat on my bed and begged me not to go through with it as I was being very unfair to my parents. They would have to look after me if I became paralysed or was brain damaged. They had lost their son and wanted to keep me as long as possible. I was devastated, and said I would talk to the chaplain, who then arrived. We talked and prayed and again he was quite wonderful. He promised he would support my parents, reassured me, and then gave me God's healing. By the time the nurse arrived to give me a sleeping tablet I was asleep. She still woke me and insisted on me having it! At 5.30 I was given a pre-med and a tablet to dry my mouth. This gave me some idea of what it must be like to die of thirst; my whole mouth swelled and my tongue seemed glued to the top of my mouth. The porters came and I was carted off to the mask and that fearful chase, only this time my heart did not pound. Instead, I went down a long corridor further and further, where it got brighter and brighter and I saw Colin. He was not a ten-week old baby but, somehow, I never expected he would be. I knew it was Colin because he looked just like the photos I had of Dad as a youth, and he spoke to me. He told me that I could not come any further and I had got to go back up the tunnel and it would all be all right. He told me God had a lot of work for me to do for him and that I was going to live for a very long time. Then I started to be sucked back up the tunnel and everything went black. When I opened my eyes all I could see was a square of ceiling and a square to the side through which faces peered. I saw my mother's face and then a nurse's. There was a terrifying rumbling noise going on all the time and every now and then an avalanche. I was in a completely opaque tent, the ward having run out of transparent ones, and the noise was the oxygen cylinder, and the avalanche was the ice moving about. Beside every tent was a tank of ice designed to keep the tents cool. These had to be topped up with fresh ice two or three times every day. It was always dreadfully hot in the tent and I was often terrified the ice had given out and they had forgotten to fill it up. I could not move my legs and one was in a splint attached to a drip giving me blood. Also, my left arm was paralysed and all I could move was my thumb and first finger. People came and did various things to me and from their conversations I gradually gathered that I had "died" on the table, been hastily returned to the ward before the operation had been finished to Sir Russell's satisfaction, and had been unconscious for over thirteen hours. Everyone seemed mightily relieved that I did not appear brain damaged. Only time would tell about everything else. My poor parents had been taken to the chapel and been told I was unlikely to make it and, as I would undoubtedly be a vegetable, to pray I died quickly. They had got to the underground when Mum remembered she had left her pools coupon on my locker so they came back. It was when Mum took a last look at me that I opened my eyes and recognised her and she called the nurse. It was some time after that before they left, and then they went to the phone box to ring all the family with the good news.

The next day I had excruciating pain in my back, which was to go on for days. They gave me Codeine, which was useless, and I suffered day and night and could think of little else. In those days they did not put in drains and it was the fluid building up from the operation. On the third day they drew the fluid off, through my back, a very painful procedure which I had to endure several times.

It was over and I was alive and each day was going to become better, but I knew that I could never go through it again. After a week I was taken out of the tent and sat out of bed in a chair. I promptly passed out and was put back to bed for another week, but not back in the tent. The feeling had come back in my legs and my left arm was starting to tingle and I could use my fingers. I had daily physiotherapy and on Christmas Day I walked for the first time, from my bed to the lunch table!

On the Monday after my operation the youngest of the children who had been in the medical ward with me, a little girl of six, went down for a Blalock op., and in the evening sister put her head into my tent and told me she was not coming back. There was no op on the Thursday but the following Monday the other girl, aged thirteen, went for a similar operation to me and did extremely well, getting over it remarkably quickly. I think they were waiting to see how I did before embarking on that op. again. She, Doris and I, all enjoyed our hospital Christmas together. Heart surgery was going forward in leaps and bounds, but it still seemed a complete lottery.

Two days before my operation a married woman had been admitted to the ward. She was to have had an operation, so far untried. She was not a blue baby but had a Mitral Stenosis, which had made her very handicapped. Her only hope for a normal life was to have heart surgery. She knew the operation carried great risks and was curious about the entire ministry I was having from the chaplain. She had also witnessed my miraculous recovery. She went home for Christmas and then came back to be another guinea pig. We talked a lot and the chaplain gave both her and her husband some instruction and then admitted them to Communion, and we all received the Sacrament together. She was also anointed the night before her operation. She never came back but I believe their newfound faith was a great consolation to her husband.

Two weeks after Christmas I went home prepared to live a normal life. The weakness in my left arm remained for some time but I was a lot better. My mother could not get over the fact that I was pink and I spent a lot of time lying flat on my back, which I could now do quite comfortably, to try and straighten my round shoulders. I had three desires, to smoke a cigarette, to ride a bike, and to swim. The first was easy to achieve and as I was still feeling the stress of such massive surgery, I started smoking quite heavily. The bike riding would come later. After about six weeks at home I was vacuuming the sitting room when I felt a terrible pain. I was rushed to the doctor and from him to hospital with pleurisy. Once again I had to be aspirated and was in hospital for another fortnight.

When I was better I wanted to start earning again. I could not go back to S.P.C.K. and Gilmore House Deaconess training college had agreed to take me to finish my I.D.C. but I would have to be there for two years as one could not start any work in the Church until one was twenty-four years old. Term did not start until October. This left the whole summer to fill.

Vida, my aunt, was very poorly. She had recently had a very painful operation, and had to spend quite a lot of time resting. She had two small children and my poor mother had been trying to help with them as well as me. It was suggested that I go and spend the summer with them in Leatherhead, to help out and look after the children. This worked extremely well and I was able to find gradually what I could do. I could take the children out and could push a pushchair. I could lift saucepans and cook dinners. I could stand on steps to clean windows. All this was quite a new world to me and I pushed myself hard, glorying in each new achievement. Vida slowly improved and we all had a wonderful summer together.

I returned to London in time to get ready to go to Gilmore House. I entered there and embarked on my new healthy life in the same month that Ines started her new life in Canada.

Rev. Margaret Freeman[3]
Great Yarmouth, England

[3] **Note**: Reverend Margaret Freeman's full story is told in her book *God's Guinea Pig*, published by iUniverse Inc, 2004.

ANGEL ON MY SHOULDER!

Sylvia Ford

I HAVE ALWAYS FELT a very strong presence of angels in my life, from the time that I was pregnant with my son. I had different organisations asking me to give up my baby. There was a very strong presence of someone guiding me, and I was adamant about keeping my baby.

Throughout raising my child, there was always someone guiding me, especially when at times it was so hard to go on.

You may wonder how I can be such a believer if you read my *True Life Story* (by Sylvia Skoog; I am now in the process of writing a sequel to it called *Misunderstandings*.)

I had a near death experience after having two surgeries close together. I had the privilege of seeing my guardian angels that let me know that it was not yet time for me to leave this earth.

I have driven a handi-bus for years and have had numerous accidents—none that were my fault. On one occasion a car ran a stop sign and hit me, throwing my vehicle into a house with such force that it moved the porch over three feet! I remained very calm and took care of my three passengers. I am thankful no-one was in the house when this happened, as it would have scared the living daylights out of them. It was much better that the house stopped me rather than the big tree that I missed by inches! When my boss got there I was in the back of the ambulance and, being the jokester that he was, he said, "Sylvia, we're not in the house moving business, you know!"—which, of course, made me laugh even though it hurt! I felt a very strong presence of someone watching over me. I could have been seriously injured and wasn't. Neither were my three passengers.

Another time a semi hit me. Again I remained calm and had this great feeling of well-being when I could have been seriously injured or killed. A lot of people don't get to tell their story after being hit by an 18-wheeler! The semi did not stop. I followed it and got the licence number, even though my bus was not in a very good shape to do this!

I thank my angels so much for watching over me. I have always sworn I have an angel on my shoulder! What do I collect? Right—angels!

* * *

More, now, about my near-death experience.

My prayers were usually in the form of anger. "Why are you doing this to me!" I would demand of God after my son, who suffers from a rare bone disorder, would break his leg or arm for the umpteenth time and had to face major surgery—again and again. There would be a few choice words in my angry outbursts. "Please leave my child alone and stop this pain!" I would scream. "He has more than his share of pain!"

I was going through some very bad times, you see. Ten years ago my father was very ill and dying, and my siblings were taking it all out of me. They accused me of not taking care of our parents properly. Out of ten children it seemed I was the one they appointed as the responsible care-giver for our parents. They were never wrong so, of course, they wouldn't want to be held responsible if anything went wrong.

Also, at this time, I needed a double surgery—one being a hysterectomy, and the other being a gall bladder operation.

The hysterectomy was done first, as I had been bleeding steadily for years and it was totally exhausting me. I did not have the greatest recovery after this surgery, and yet the surgeon wanted to go on to the gall bladder surgery just about right away. My gynaecologist did not want him to do it for at least six months. The surgeon insisted, nevertheless, saying this would be a very simple operation, and that he would do it by laproscopy and I would be out of hospital in twenty-four hours.

I should have known by now that things don't run that smoothly for me! They went ahead with the surgery and I have never been sicker in my life! I found out later that they had cut the pancreatic duct. I was bleeding internally and was totally infected.

After five days of not caring whether I lived or died, my husband came in and told them he wanted to see some doctors right away! ("Right NOW!" he demanded!). Well, that started the action. Within a half hour they had me on an I.V. with heavy doses of antibiotics going through my system. They also moved me into a private room at no extra charge. The ward they had me in before had one bathroom and a lady with staff infection. My husband told them to get me out of there right away—"Right NOW!"—again, not mincing his words!

It was about four days later that I saw my angels. They were in the form of my best friend Billy and Granny—who had some time ago departed this earth. They had an aura of light around them. They were a distance away, and kept coming in closer. They had a beautiful smile on both of their faces. Then they started fading and disappeared.

After I was well enough to think this wonderful experience over, I realised they were telling me they loved me—but that it was not my time to go with them yet.

I am no longer afraid of death. It was the most beautiful and amazing experience that I have ever had!

Sylvia Ford[4]
Alberta, Canada

---

[4] Note: Sylvia Ford's full story is told in her book *True Life Story* by Sylvia Skoog, published by iUniverse Inc, 2003.

JESUS WAS THERE—And I did not know it!

Carol MacKenzie

I WAS BORN IN 1965 into a loving Christian family—
the only child of Ken and Isobel Adams. I was brought
up in Dunoon, in Scotland, and attended the Baptist Church
with my parents all of my childhood until I was fifteen.

Up until then I had done what I was asked and didn't
question it. As I became older I realised I wanted to fit in
with my peers who didn't go to church. So I stopped going
to church then and didn't return until I was much older.

A Mission had come to Dunoon Baptist Church. As my
dad was a deacon he was asked if some of the mission
could stay with them. This was not a problem and a Captain
Anderson and his daughter came to stay. I don't remember
when they came, but it was when I was twenty—and by
now I had my own social life with my friends and was
planning to go out that night. It was Friday night, the start
of the weekend! Mum and Dad unexpectedly had to go
away for the weekend. I was going out with my friends but,
as it happened, my friends cancelled their plans, so when
Captain Anderson's daughter asked me to come to the
mission show that night I had no reason not to.

It was that night I gave my life to the Lord Jesus Christ!
Now, when I look back, I can see the Lord's hand at work,
though it was not plain sailing from then on. I remember
the joy I had that morning after the night before, so to

speak. I realised I could start all over again—my sins were forgiven, I was washed clean…

But it didn't last very long. My new-found joy had no depth of character. I started to feel 'embraced' or restricted by a Christ-centred lifestyle—in a sense I felt I was not able to live up to my expectations of what a Christian should be like; and so I drifted away from the Lord.

When Ruaridh was born in 1990 I was filled with that joy again and decided to rededicate my life to the Lord. My husband and I decided to join the Local Church of Scotland in Dalgetty Bay were we were living.

We moved to Almondbank in1991 and our membership moved with us. I attended the local Church, but after trying very hard to fit in found that with a small child I needed more for Ruaridh.

I was directed to Perth Baptist Church by a Gideon friend of my dad's whose son had been appointed the new pastor there, Rev. Charles Young. When I went I was astounded at how family oriented they were, and how many children there were. I was delighted, and so was Ruaridh!

I had been regularly attending P.B.C for about a year when I became pregnant. Kirsty arrived safely on Sunday 4th September, 1994, three weeks early. She was blessed in P.B.C around the age of six months.

It was about this time I started noticing changes with my left hand. I had a shake and found I had difficulty walking because of my bad balance. We were blessed with a very good neighbour, Mrs Helen Clark. I asked her to help me with looking after Kirsty changing her nappy, bathing her and binging her downstairs. I still didn't know what was wrong with me. Time went by and I finally got a diagnosis. I had M.S.—Multiple Sclerosis. It was 4th August, 1995—a date that will never leave me, one year after it began.

The attacks were now slowing down and I could do a lot more for Kristy. Helen didn't need to come in quite so often now and I began to gain more confidence, walking around with Kristy in my arms. I decided one day to wear a new denim skirt I had and a pair of black boots. The boots were quite heavy, but I decided to wear them nevertheless. Kristy was dressed and ready to go, so I picked her up in my arms and we went downstairs.

As I started to go down the thirteen stairs I realised the boots were far too heavy and the skirt far too long for tackling the stairs, especially with my baby daughter in my arms—but it was too late when I remembered. It was about the fourth step down when things became very difficult. I remember stumbling and not being able to grab the rail that was on my left side (my weak side). I was terrified. I could see the bottom of the stairs getting closer all the time as I tried to find my feet and tried to grab the rail—all at the same time. We were now about three steps from the bottom. I could see the curling stones and the wooden runner in front of the hardwood door—all were dangers, and I had to make a decision. I would save Kristy as best I could. So I stuck out my elbows and held Kristy close to me and closed my eyes…

We landed with a bump. Kristy's head hit the runner but, apart from that, we were okay. I remember crying and shaking with fright and feeling Kristy all over. We went into the kitchen for a cold cloth for Kristy's head.

I only told Ranald and Ruaridh that we had fallen down the stairs and nothing else because I was so ashamed of my choice of clothes.

We went to church that Sunday as usual. When going up the ramp when I was stopped by Mrs Muriel Murray. "I've to give this to you, Carol," she said and gave me a poem.

As I read the poem I realised Jesus had never left me. Here is the poem:

HE WAS THERE

Jesus heard when you prayed last night,
He talked with God about you;
Jesus was there when you fought that fight,
He is going to bring you through.

Jesus knew when you shed those tears,
But you did not weep alone;
For the burden you thought too heavy to bear,
He made His very own.

Jesus Himself was touched by that trial,
Which you could not understand;
Jesus stood by as you almost fell,
And lovingly grasped your hand.

The tears ran down my face! I could read no
more… He was there! He had never left me… all
the heartache… all the tears… all the years… and
when I fell he was there too!

Jesus cared when you bore that pain;
Indeed, he bore it too;
He felt each pang, each ache in your heart,
Because of His love for you.

Jesus was grieved when you doubted His love,
But He gave you grace to go on;
Jesus rejoiced as you trusted Him,
The only trustworthy One.

His Presence shall ever be with you,
No need to be anxious or fret;
Wonderful Lord! He was there all the time,
He has never forsaken you yet.

The poem was written by Mrs Nell Hawkins, 8 Vienna court, Durban Road, Old swan, Liverpool, L13 5SY.

This little poem changed my life. I now saw where his hand had been directing my life. He directed me again, using his word in 1 Timothy 6:12:

Fight the good fight of the faith.
take hold of the eternal life to which you
were called when you made your good
confession in the presence of many witnesses.

On the 17th August, 1997, I was baptised in Perth Baptist Church.

I did what he wanted me to do. In being baptised in Christ I died to self. I am still dying to self—it is one of the hardest things to do on your own.

But I'm not on my own. Jesus is here, guiding me, showing me his way to go and how to go about it.

Carol MacKenzie
North Laggan, Scotland

A KNOCK IN TIME

Janet Watson

IT WAS THE AUTUMN OF 1991, a Saturday night, about 10.40. My son Jon had just rang me to tell me that he couldn't get a lift home from his work about seven miles away in Brigg.

Jon worked in a residential home for people with learning difficulties. He was twenty at the time. My eldest son Chris lived down in Newbury, in Berks. I had my daughter Lena, who was fifteen, at home, but she was staying the night with friends. So I sat alone in a dark house when Jon's call came. He explained that no matter how hard he had tried, he couldn't get a lift home, and that there were no taxis available.

The world crowded in on me and I knew I had just passed breaking point. I had been banging my face against the wall and only eating toast once or twice a week for a long time. All I did was sit and try and rock my deep-rooted pain out of me. I did not want to know my children who were and still are the centre of my being.

For the next few minutes my whole miserable life came into focus—my father's wanderings when I was growing up, the many times he had left my mum and his children—was it five or six?

In my desire to be loved, my need to belong to someone, I went through three disastrous marriages; one was fraught with jealousy and betrayal, the other with physical pain and abuse, while the third involved my children in circumstances still too painful to speak of.

As I sat there my fourth marriage had just ended because my husband wouldn't pay bills and took my wages from working at William Booth House in Hull off me, leaving me begging him for a pair of shoes, for my only pair had holes in the soles. It wasn't the drink or horses that possessed him, but his insatiable addiction to the gambling allure of the one-armed bandits.

I had just left Hull and returned to my family in Scunthorpe. Foolishly I turned to a man twelve years younger than me, a man I met at work. I didn't know at the time I met him that he had served time in prison and would be back there within a year.

How could I stop this? How could this cycle of misery, of giving my all and getting nothing in return, be broken?

It was at that moment I decided to take my life.

My son had an air pistol in the drawer in the kitchen and I decided it was as good a way as any. I walked into the kitchen with the sole purpose of taking my life. I was determined nothing would stop me! I loaded the gun and put it into my mouth.

At that moment there was a knock at the door.

How stupid of someone to knock! It was 11 o' clock at night and the house was in pitch darkness—and there was a gun in my mouth. What a time to knock!

After switching on the Hall light I opened the front door. A young man, between 25 and 35, stood there. He asked me if I knew of a family that lived down the road.

After telling him I had just moved in and didn't know anybody, he asked me to go to the gate with him to give him directions back into the town centre. I gave him these and he looked down at what I presumed was his watch and said goodnight.

As I watched him walk down the street I thought, why *my* house? There were plenty of my neighbours who were still up, their houses all ablaze with lights on. And as I watched him he suddenly evaporated into nothing!

I went back in and looked at the clock—just gone eleven—and I thought, "Somebody doesn't want me to do this." But I was resolved and went back into the kitchen—I had made up my mind and was on a mission of self-annihilation!

I don't know how long I stood there, but the next thing I knew Jon was knocking at the door and the gun was in my hand. When I let him in he explained to me that a man had come up to him at two minutes past eleven and said, "You're wanted at home!" The man had accompanied Jon and it took them seven minutes to get home. When I opened the door only Jon was there.

Jon saw the pistol and guessed what I was trying to do. He wasn't happy, to say the least! I stormed up the stairs and, in my arrogance, shouted to God: "All right, God! If you want me, fetch me!"

Eventually he did. I gave my life to the Lord in the summer of 1990 at a praise party in Scunthorpe. My walk with the Lord has not been an easy one, but I have overcome my demons and learned to give everything, including myself. With the Lord's help I have overcome agoraphobia, and I hope to walk with the Lord into my sunset—and beyond.

Janet Watson
Hull, England

TOUCHED BY A COW

A Testimony by Kit Calvert, as told by Pat Dean

*(This testimony is based on the actual
testimony narrated by the late Kit Calvert,
OBE, a well-known and well-respected
figure in Hawes, North Yorkshire. The
interview was recorded on tape and later
transcribed by Pat Dean who, for dramatic
purposes, has recast the testimony here in
the form of a dialogue between Kit (Matt)
Calvert and a young visitor to the Dales.)*

FAITH to the openhearted Matt Calvert and his friends
was an intensely personal matter—one which was
approached in such a down to earth, matter of fact manner
that it seemed custom-made for their way of life. Men who
walk hand in hand with nature through the seasons can
accept the mystery of the miracles, for they see them at
every turn on their lives.

As we turned into the yard, the work dogs came darting
across to see us. They were only just losing their wariness
of me, for in their eyes I was of course a stranger. Matt,
however, was clearly their mentor and I could imagine how
in the first few months of their lives he would have talked
to them, played with them, already having the trust of their
mother, and begun in this way to train them for the work
they must do. High on the moors on a Sunday morning,
with the piping calls of moorland birds for company, the
dogs had to react sharply to the calls of 'Bye bye' and

'Way bye' to bring the sheep round to the shepherd so that he may look them over and be sure the flock is well on its lofty summer pasture.

As the dogs threw themselves on the heather, smelling of peat and panting quickly from their exertions, Matt would look into their eyes and down into their very soul, telling them they had done well or were becoming lazy. Each seemed to know what was being said and moved their bodies in answer. Just like everything else on the farm, the dogs had to earn their keep, but with this Matt had more than a working relationship.

After master and animals had made their greeting, we turned towards the cottage, for Kate and left us a cold pie so that Matt and I could have a lazy supper. I knew too that Jack was going to be busy with his accounts and Kate wanted to catch up on some letter writing. Matt drew up his chair and I put the food on the table. Through the little side window I could see the darkening shadow of a wood on the valley side and the occasional flicker of car lights as a vehicle drove over the road that climbed steeply before falling equally sharply to the next dale. The meal finished, I replenished the teapot and we smiled contentedly at each other while Matt contemplated his Sunday attire, looking slightly less severe now that his waistcoat was unfastened.

'I feel strange now if I don't go to chapel or church on a Sunday,' he began. 'But it wasn't always so.'

I smiled encouragingly. 'How so?'

'It's something of an intimate tale and one very few people know about, but my spiritual life was awakened by a cow.'

'A cow!' I laughed.

Matt nodded, unperturbed. 'When I was a teenager I was very fond of argument, and religion was always one of the best subjects. Once when there had been a revival meeting up at Gayle, quite a number of young folk were influenced by a couple of lady evangelists -- influenced to such an extent that their lives had definitely been moulded by that three-week mission. But it didn't make any impression on me at all. In fact, it went the other way! I well remember one night during this mission some of the lads who had been converted were resting in a hut from their work on the roads. It was a wild day so I went in to see them and they were reading the Bible and they started on me. I went in like a terrier and started to fire questions at them and give 'em a real good hammering in me own way! At the finish, one of 'em says, "We ought to have thee on *our* side!"

' "Aye, you should! But you've got something on to get me," I challenged.

'They said they would try.

' "Well, you have the weapon in your hands," I went on. "You say prayers can move mountains. Never mind the mountains! Try and move *me*!"

'They tried, but nothing came of it. Anyway, time passed and the mission finished and I bought a cow with a view to winning the Christmas prize show at the auction mart. Now you know what my wages were in those days. I hadn't a lot of money; but I'd saved sufficient to buy this cow for £33 from a cattle dealer. £33 was a lot of money to men. It was a good cow, but it had one little fault. It had a little bit of a growth on a front knee and I knew very well it couldn't win the Christmas prize show with this fault; so I asked the local cow doctor if he would take it off!

'He looked at it and said he might, but it would be rather dangerous as it was on the end of a muscle. Any slip and she could be lamed.

'I asked the vet and he looked at it and said he would rather not touch it. Anyway, I found another vet, a broken-down one, and asked him if he could take it off. "I'll take its head off if thou wants it," he said. I said I didn't *want* the head off, just the little bit of growth. So he decided he would do it.

'So he came and then just as he was going to start, I thought about what those other two experts had told me. So I said to him: "You'll be careful, now. They say if you slip at all you can let the leg down if you cut it."

'He said, "Who says I'm going to cut it!" And he brought out this instrument which was a chanin inside a bit of pipe, and he wrapped it round the lump. Then he just pulled and it shot off! He stitched it up, but the next morning I saw something had happened. The cow was bleeding profusely from this wound.

'Anyway, I then got veterinary assistance to try and stop it -- and he stopped the wound. But septic set in and by Sunday the cow was in agony. The leg was nearly the thickness of the body! The cow was in terrible pain with blood poisoning, when an old man called round to see it. The man said, "That'll cap [teach] thee! You young 'uns, you know more than old 'uns. You'll learn your lesson in time." All my worldly goods were tied up in that cow and I was a bit disturbed. Anyway, he gave me a good thrashing talk for doing such tricks when I had been advised by reputed vets to leave it alone.

'That was Sunday morning. In the afternoon I went down from home at Burtersett to see this cow that was in a barn at Hawes. I was going to try to feed her and I was very depressed because the old feller had told me she'd be dead in a few days. She'd slip her calf and the blood poisoning would set in right through her system, he'd said.

'On the way across the fields, I saw a stamp on the flags and why I picked it up I don't know; but when I look at it, it must have been given to some bairns at Sunday School and there was a little flower and text on it. It said, "Have faith in God."

'I thought I might as well, for I didn't have much faith in myself or my cow. I walked along to the barn and heard her moaning long before I got there. Every moan struck right through me, saying it was my fault. Before I knew where I was, I was in the hay mew praying! "Lord, do summat for cow! Either cure her or put her out of her misery; but for mercy's sake, don't let me hear this moaning any more!"

'I kept talking like that to myself, or to God, I don't know. "If you can cure her, Lord, she'll not be used for my glory."

'All at once it dawned on me. I thought to myself, "You always swore there was no God! What the deuce are you doing praying?" I wrestled with myself and the outcome was that I submitted that I *must* believe there was a God. I repeated my promise and strange to say I never heard that moaning anymore. Next day she seemed a bit better, and the next day she was a lot better. Sunday came round again and so did this old feller.

' "Well, this caps the devil!" he exclaimed. "She should have been under the sod pushing up daisies. Whatever's happened?" I gave him a wry smile, like, but didn't tell him.

'Anyway, she carried on improving and I had to sell her at the Christmas show, for she was the only cow I had and I was paying for her keep. The day before she had to go, she was looking her best and I remembered my promise. "I promised God I would not use her for my own glory, and I won't -- I won't! He put her right!"

'I was yard man at the mart at that time and when I had brought the cow up for sale, I got on with some jobs well away from the top ring where the selling was going to be. After a bit a friend came down with my cow and asked me where I'd been. I said I'd been working in another yard. "Why, thou nearly lost first prize!" he said.

' "I didn't ask for first prize."

' "But you bought cow to win with!"

' "I did once, but I wasn't bothering."

'"Thou *wasn't bothering*! What was thou *thinkin'* about! Anyway, never bother about that. I saw thou'd been left out so I took her up and she's won first prize! She's won the cup!"

' "Well, I never took her," I said, and then I was joined by the old man who'd prophesised my cow would be pushing up daisies. "I said she'd win, now we're joining. How much to join?" he asked. You'll know, lad, that that was the way of bidding up the price on an animal beyond what folks would pay normally. I said I wasn't going to and of course he wanted to know what for.

' "For private reasons."

' "You promised me you would join when you bought her if she did well!"

' "I maybe promised that, but we're not joining."

'He persisted, then said: "I'll tell thee summat then, if thou wants to know! I've been talking with the judge who gave it first prize and he wants her for Darlington show. He'll give £70 for her! But he says she'll not make about £50 or £55 unless somebody put's her up."

'He persisted and persisted and then said I'd always promised him something if she did well. "I did and I will," I said, and I went into my pocket and gave him £3 and told him to take it and let me alone and that it didn't matter if she only made £30. So he did and as I went into the auction ring with the cow, I put my stick across and tapped him on the shoulder and said, "I'm watching thee. This cow is to be sold genuinely. If thou bids at that cow by a nod or a wink I'll expose you to the whole crowd." He said: "Thou needn't watch me. I'll be out of the spot."—and he went out.

'The cow made £50. Joining would have got her to £70. She went to Northallerton and won there and then she went to Darlington and won second prize. But to me, I won my soul.'

Looking suddenly tired, but with his eyes shining, Matt tilted back his chair and smiled at me. My eyes were shining too, but with a touch of dampness, for this had been an open window right through to Matt's heart and I guessed that very few people, probably even my father, had ever heard of how his faith had been founded; and founded well, for it was never found lacking and I knew it was as solid as bedrock. For a while there was a silence broken only by the ticking of the clock while I pondered on the tremendous feeling of steady certainty which must come from such a faith. No wonder such people inspired trust in animals and children, who also had the eyes to see and the ears to hear. They seemed to have a direct line to the sense most mortals lose before being aware of its presence but which is sometimes to be found among the elderly. Do we fight it down in middle life, or is it just overwhelmed in the rush to prove that activity is action? A few, no, an infinitely few people, retain the link all their lives. Was simplicity of outlook a cause or result?

The riddle was too hard for me just now.

ALL THINGS WORK TOGETHER FOR GOOD...

Dr Robert Peprah-Gyamfi

IN OCTOBER 1984 I began my medical studies at the Hannover Medical School in Germany. Before moving to Hannover, I spent two years in the then West Berlin as an Asylum seeker from Ghana. During my stay there I worshipped at the American Lutheran Church in Berlin. It was during the cold war. Germany was divided as a result of World War II. Several American soldiers were stationed in West Berlin. The American Lutheran Church was not part of the military establishment but rather served the English speaking American civilian community as well as other English-speaking residents of the divided city from various parts of the globe.

After I had matriculated with the medical school of the northern German city, I applied for a room in one of the three hostels serving students registered with that institution of higher learning. Because there was no vacancy at that time, my name was placed on the waiting list. With the help of Pastor Kawalla, then the superintendent pastor of the German Lutheran Church for the Hannover-North district, I found temporary accommodation in a hostel serving mostly students of a Theological Seminary not far from the medical school. I learnt on moving to my new accommodation that not very far from the building was another facility that served as refuge for delinquent teenagers who could no longer live with their parents.

To facilitate my movement and also save the money I would otherwise have spent on going by public transport, I bought a new bicycle. My silver-coloured bike eventually became my good companion, enabling me to reach the lecture hall on time, helping me transport my shopping basket home and also taking me to the church where I worshipped, which happened to be located some five kilometres from the hostel.

Like anyone else living in the hostel, I chained my bike every evening to a special stand that had been erected near the building for that purpose.

Barely three months after acquiring the bike, I left my room one morning to collect my bike for a ride to the medical school, not suspecting anything. I had as usual calculated my time so as to be punctual for lectures—but to my utter dismay, my faithful companion was nowhere to be seen! In my desperation I went about searching the compound around the building in the hope that perhaps someone had deposited it somewhere after using it for a riding tour. Apparently someone among the delinquent teenagers had visited the stand during the night and made away with my good-looking bike.

At that time I belonged to a Bible study and prayer group led by Pastor Kawalla. One of the members of the group, on learning about my situation, presented me with a replacement. It was an old worn-out bike that could not in any way compare with the stolen one. Nevertheless, the fact that I had the means that could at least still make me independent of public transport was consoling enough to me.

A few days later, I rode it to church. With the help of a metal chain I fastened it to a lamppost on the street a few metres from the church building. After a lively church service I headed for the old bike to pick it up for my ride home. What did I realise? That one, too, was nowhere to be seen! I just couldn't believe my eyes! How on earth would anyone want to steal anything like an old bike like that!

So—two lost bikes within a period less than two weeks! Somehow, I was tempted to be angry with God. In particular, the fact that I had lost the second bike while attending church was difficult for me to swallow.

But I was not someone who was new to the Faith. Over a period of about sixteen years to that day, I had experienced the working of the Great Redeemer in my life. Over that period of time He had turned several seemingly dead-end situations in my life around, in some instances in ways that had beaten my ordinary human understanding.

So, once the shock of my loss had abated and I stood there before the lamppost where I had fastened my bike a few hours earlier, I could only wonder what He had in store for me this time round.

But what was I to do? Although the city of Hannover boasts of a well-functioning public transport service—commuter trains, streetcars, buses, etc—for reasons already mentioned, I preferred going by bike. My meagre financial resources would not permit me to buy a brand new bike again. Even if I had the funds, the events of the last several days had led me to a situation where I did not want to invest a substantial amount of money for that purpose.

In the end, acquiring another second-hand bike on the flea market was the alternative I wanted to consider. Before I resorted to that, however, an idea occurred to me—to call Gary, the pastor of the American Church in Berlin, to inform him of my predicament and request him to make an announcement in church the following Sunday to the effect that if, possibly, there was a member of the church who was ready to dispose of an old bike, perhaps wasting away in the cellar or backyard of his or her home…

Gary promised to do as requested.

A few days later I received a message from Berlin to the effect that one of the members of the church was willing to present me with a bike! Another member of the church who happened to be travelling to Hannover—a city located about three hundred kilometres to the west of Berlin—agreed to bring it along.

The sight of the gift from Berlin has humbled me to this day.

I was not being presented with an ordinary bike, but the type that in my opinion deserves the accolade 'extraordinary'! It was a never used and elegant bright red coloured six-gear sports-bike! It may well have been worth three times the value of my first stolen bike. That anyone would be willing to give it for free was beyond my comprehension.

The couple that donated it served with the US Military in Berlin. They had brought the bike with them to Germany, thinking they would need it. That was, however, not the case. Their tour of duty in Berlin was just about to come to an end and they had been deliberating on how to dispose of it before their return home. They did not hesitate a moment after hearing the announcement to donate it to a person they had heard many good things about. I must say, though, that up to that time, they did not belong to the group of church members to whom I had close contact with. For the next several days—and even up till now—the mysterious workings of the Lord that led me to the amazing bike has continued to baffle me and occupy my mind.

Over the next several years my bright red sports bike carried me over several hundred kilometres as I went about my daily life in the northern German city that boasted about half a million residents.

Whenever I ponder over the events that led me to the bike, the passage of scripture that comes to my mind is:

"And we know that all things work together for good to them that love God, to them who are called according to his purpose."
(Romans 8:28—King James Version.)

True, the Christian may sometimes go through circumstances in life that might lead that person to wonder how in the midst of that particular state of affairs all things *could* work together for his/her good. How could Joseph, for example, discern at the time when he was thrown into the pit, when he was sold to Egypt, yes indeed when he was cast into prison for standing by principle and not giving into temptation to commit adultery with the wife of his master, that all things would indeed work together for his good?

To you, dear child of God who might seem to be in a no-way-out or no-win situation, I say this: since we are serving the Lord who knows the beginning from the end, and the end from the beginning, my prayer is that you will draw inspiration from my humble experience, which, though it may seem banal in comparison with the mountains of problems before you, will help you to draw inspiration and wait for the mysterious hands of the Lord to draw you to safety.

Indeed, my experience from following the Lord has left me in no doubt that all things work together for good for those that love God, to them that are called to his purpose—if not in this life, then at the latest when we shall see Him face to face.

Dr Robert Peprah-Gyamfi
Loughborough, England

JUSTINE ANGEL

Colin Edwards

IT WAS THE MID-1990'S and my wife and I were in one of those deep troughs that life seems to produce from time to time. It was a classic story of unemployment and shortage of funds. Unless I could create some income, the car would have to be sold. Our house had already been repossessed a couple of years earlier, wiping out all our savings and we were living in a rented flat. Instead of taking the easy route of giving in to depression, I decided to create my own home-based business. It would be a zero cost operation where I would contact everyone that I knew to launch an affordable PR service for small companies and people in professional practice.

My usually creative imagination failed to deliver a catchy name and memorable logo, two ingredients that would surely help the venture's launch. I covered sheets of scrap paper with possible ideas, but none of them fitted the bill.

Later that week I was invited to visit a nearby town— one that we had often driven through but rarely stopped at. As I parked the car I noticed an obviously newly opened charity shop.

I homed in on the books. I reached for a slim paperback, *Angel Therapy*. It looked brand new and was priced at 10p. Almost immediately I dropped it. That is an understatement. It almost flew out of my hand and landed, face downwards in a box of bric-a-brac on the floor. Bending to retrieve it, I was intrigued by a bit of grubby brown wood sticking up at the back of the box. I moved some junk to unearth it and found that it was an art deco style, carved, wooden angel!

I asked the price. "You can have it dear," the assistant said. "I cannot think where it came from. We only opened this morning for the first time, but I don't remember seeing it before." I paid for the book and then, with book and angel in a carrier bag, we left.

It was one of those strange November days when the afternoon sky, heading rapidly towards dusk, was blanketed with heavy, unbroken, dark and brooding cloud. Suddenly there was a break in the cloud. It only lasted a few seconds but was right in line with the low sun, which cast a beam like a stage spotlight across the street. The beam was so focused that the shops either side of the charity shop were still in shadow while the shop we had visited was bathed in a brilliant golden glow. It hit me full on. Within a matter of seconds it had vanished.

That evening, whilst my wife was out, I set to work with fine sandpaper and cleaned up the wooden angel. I found the can of gold paint that had been around since we painted an old vase some weeks previously and gave her a bright new coat.

When my wife returned she immediately noted the smell of paint and then looked at what I had been doing. The golden angel was propped up under a table lamp and looked...well, sort of magical. I said, "While I was cleaning her, I invented the name for my business. You are now about to sleep with the managing director of The Justine Angel PR Organisation!"

The very next day I had a phone call from a friend. "I have this pal at work that needs some PR stuff—I immediately thought of you. Would you like to give him a call?" This was the first of what was to become a steady stream of income-generating assignments.

A few days later, I felt that the lady in the charity shop would be interested to see how the angel had turned out. I parked in the same slot as before. I left the car park on foot, exactly as before. The shop was empty. Its windows were painted out with whitewash. I enquired at the estate agency next door.

"Odd," they said. "We don't know who they were. They were a strange couple, because they both dressed in white and, although they had blond hair, they weren't at all washed out looking. In fact, we commented at the time about how they could look so warm and colourful all in white. They collected the key from us in the morning and gave it back in the afternoon and we never saw them again." They continued: "We remember it well because, just as they left us we thought there had been an accident. There was this almighty crackle of lightning and a crash of thunder. One minute they were there, the next they had vanished. Funny, the storm we were expecting never happened. We did try to contact them to return the deposit they paid on the shop and to thank them for leaving it so much cleaner than it had been before. All our other paperwork was where it should be, but we couldn't find any record of them anywhere. All we can remember is that they were in their late 30's and had amazingly brilliant smiles all the time they were here."

You must draw your own conclusions.

Although I have a keen interest in advertising and media matters, I have been unable to discover any company that may have used this angel as a brand, logo, or trademark. She now hangs on the wall, in pride of place above my desk... a constant reminder of the power of the unseen. She may be only 18" tall and 12" from wingtip to wingtip, but she sure created an impact in my life.

Why Justine? That is another equally strange story that may be told one day.

Colin Edwards[5]
Bromley, England

---

[5] Colin Edwards is the author of *The Star Process*, iUniverse 2005, ISBN 0-595-3661-7.

GUARDIAN ANGELS[6]

Inez Randolph

HAVE YOU NOTICED that sometimes certain people, be it family members or otherwise, give you unexpected advice or ask you to do things that you hadn't planned but that turn out to be beneficial to you? Further still, we often feel the presence of someone watching over us, making sure we are safe, and this feeling of having someone close is always there, especially when we are in tricky or dangerous situations. This presence reassures us and makes us feel that we are never alone. Sometimes, too, certain people unknown to us might say something to comfort us or do something for us that we needed at a particular time. These people or "presences" are what I refer to as guardian angels.

Heaven and hell, my grandma says, are here on earth and nowhere else. To this, I adhere. Besides, to underline this we often qualify a horrible event in our lives as "living hell". Heaven is also used to describe the intense feeling of joy and happiness we experience in certain moments in our lives. That is when, I guess, we talk about being in seventh heaven. In the same way, I believe that angels are not extraterrestrial white beings with wings. I think angels are human beings like you and I who come in all forms and sizes from different races, backgrounds and ages. These people could be family or otherwise who manifest

---

[6] Reprinted from *True Life Reflections: A compilation of short essays and poems* by Inez Randolph. iUniverse 2004, ISBN: 0-595-33217-X.

themselves at exactly the right time and the right place when we need them. Sometimes they are with us for a long time and other times they just come to accomplish a particular task and leave. Whatever the case, however, I am convinced they are God sent.

In my case, I have met people in strange places in unusual situations in different countries who have talked to me and advised me about personal and professional problems that have saved my life. I have travelled quite a bit and, apart from being looked after at airports, I have had wonderful people look after me in various circumstances with no questions asked—people who were just there to help me when I thought all was lost. The funny thing is, I seem to have a guardian angel in all the places I've been in. I've often wondered if I have one in each country! I have also felt the presence of someone watching over me especially when I am afraid. I guess this is also my guardian angel at work.

I don't know about you, but I have come to the conclusion that all guardian angels are good Samaritans. The good thing is that, if we look beyond the physical aspect and appearance, we might just find our guardian angel right beside us.

Inez Randolph
Accra, Ghana

FROM FEAR TO VICTORY

Janey Menzies

TURNING DOWN the narrow bumpy dusty road of Chaisa presented my first face to face encounter with the poverty of Africa. Nothing could have prepared me for what met my eyes. This was no movie, it was my world colliding with the reality of theirs. My abundance compared to their lack. The children smiled as they played in the dust, oblivious to their needs and the needs of those around them. They knew no better life.

On this, my first experience, I had little idea of the life that lay ahead of me amongst the African people and that this place of poverty would soon become a second home to me. I was also unaware of the prejudices that lay in me and how God was leading me to step across and break them.

As we continued down the road that twisted between the houses in the protection and comfort of our car, dust and bumps worsened as did the anxiety in my heart! Nervously I follow Pastor Mark into this small and makeshift looking church, which to my surprise was filled with Africans joyfully worshiping God! We were invited to sit at the front but my deep dislike of attention forced me to weave my way to the back and squeeze in alongside the Africa women. The joy and warmth of the Africans worshiping God was strikingly different to anything I had previously experienced. But it soon became a familiar place for me to connect with God, in both joy and intimacy. The great freedom compels you to join in the clapping, dancing, shouting, all deep expressions of genuine praise to God. Pastor Mark went on to preach a powerful message on healing, with many going forward at the end, and coming away with testimonies of miracles. How God moved to meet the needs of these spiritually (and physically for some) hungry people! Sitting amongst the ladies was an experience in itself. The lack of space on the bench meant that the lady next to me squeezed up tight, totally unaware she was overstepped my British comfort zone! (In her mind it was a privilege!)

On later visits to that same church I realised that sitting at the front was really the norm for visitors, and my sitting in the crowd would have caused more heads to turn than would have happened had I sat where I was supposed to sit! It was the crippling fear of man that had gripped my life and overcoming this fear is the victory of my story.

Growing up in Scotland, I inherited the common Scottish trait of low self-esteem, worsened by the usual increase of self-awareness that develops in teenagers. I left school with a great education, but with zero self-confidence and avoided speaking in public at all cost. This same attitude followed me to university and even into the workplace where I worked as a physiotherapist. Only moments of bravery would descend on me at church when the floor would be opened for testimonies and I would face my fears to testify to what my great God had done in my life.

It was after three years working in Perth Royal Infirmary that I knew I could no longer run from this strong desire in me, and I had to step out of the boat to do what God was calling me to do. With no idea what that really meant or where it would lead, I sought out mission organizations I could serve with, using physiotherapy to help the poor and suffering in this world. To my surprise no opportunities opened before me, and as I questioned the Lord to His direction and will for my life, he whispered into my spirit,

"Go to Bible College." "What, Lord? Me, go to Bible College?" I questioned, and added, "I am not spiritual enough!" Every excuse was not going to stand against the will of God for my life, of course. I knew I must go and so nine months later, I left my full-time job, my friends, my church, my family, to head to Bible School in England.

Sitting under the guidance of Apostle Colin Urquhart and the power of the word of God transformed me! The passion for the lost, the yearning for his presence and the fire for God's kingdom grew strongly in me! I was changed, but the strongholds of fear remained in my thinking.

Following the Lord's clear direction and will for my life, He led me to Africa to join an evangelism team. Not physiotherapy, and not what I really expected, but it was what moved my heart.

It was only three days after my first visit with Pastor Mark that I headed back to Chiasa, but this time I wasn't there to listen, but rather to preach. The ladies I had squeezed up with on the benches we're now the ones sitting staring at me. Almost sick with fear, I prayed, "Dear lord, I cannot do this, but I know you can! Please help me and be gloried in everything I do." This prayer became, and has remained, the bottom line of who I have become and the key I would give, and have given, to my walk with the Lord.

I took my diligently prepared notes and spoke out almost word for word what I believed God had given me to say—a message about who we are in Christ, one of the teachings from Bible School that I knew I could regurgitate most easily. The ladies listened, interjecting the odd "Amen" to encourage me, and my goal was twofold—Lord be glorified, and when can I sit down?! Twenty minutes later I finished. Great relief—*that* it was over! But unfortunately the journey was only just beginning! Despite all I learnt at Bible School, it did not prepare me for the battle in my mind. An onslaught of negative thoughts persisted in trying to beat me to my core. Every reason was given that I was useless at preaching, and why would anyone want to listen to me and what do I have to offer anyway?!

Those first experiences and much of my first year in Africa remain etched in memory as I began to take my first steps into who I was created to be and what God had destined me to do. It was 2003, and the work of the crusade ministry took us from city to city in southern Africa, preaching the Gospel. Evangelist Christopher Alam preached in the crusades and directed the ministry. Our job as the team was to train the believers from the local churches in preparation for the crusade. Although I knew that preaching would be a part of the work, I hadn't fully considered how big a part it was to play. By the end of the first year, I had had enough. Every time I spoke the devil attacked with such ferociousness—it was soul destroying.

I clearly remember Christopher Alam saying "I want you to do more preaching"—and the voice in my head clearly saying, "But I am so useless, you have got it wrong!"

Well, he hadn't got it wrong, but the devil was wrong! God opened so many doors of opportunity to preach and teach. I stayed with the crusade ministry for eight years, and each year a greater anointing and grace would flow through my life to the spiritually hungry souls of Africa. The fear and chains of fear slowly fell off, and the power of His word would bring life to those to whom I preached.

The evangelist Christopher Alam had a powerful testimony of salvation from being brought up as a Muslim. He was called by God to preach the Gospel and anointed to pray for the sick. The crusades were characterized by large crowds—5,000 to 20,000 people, the main focus being to preach the Gospel and to pray for the sick, as Jesus had commanded us to do, which was his great commission. It was my great privilege to witness at first hand hundreds and thousands of miracles. Deaf ears being opened is the most common miracle I have seen, but I also witnessed sight being restored to blind eyes and the lame walking, and many more.

I remember a crusade in another compound of Lusaka called George. During the afternoon children's crusade, four elderly people walked over two kilometres to receive prayer for their sick bodies. They had heard that God was doing miracles and decided to seek God for the answer to their problems. They sat and waited on myself and Svetla, my fellow missionary, as we finished our children's crusade. Tired and harassed from a hectic afternoon with the children, Svetla and I prayed for those elderly folk to be cured of their ailments. To our joy and amazement, all four were healed! A deaf ear was opened, partial eyesight was restored, a stroke inflicted body was released to walk with pain-free movement, and symptoms from a heart problem disappeared. All four sat with glee at how the Lord had touched their bodies. They decided to stay on for the evening crusade when they lifted their hands to receive Jesus into their hearts. What a joy to be used by God for his kingdom power to touch and transform lives!

Each crusade ran for five or six nights during which time we would hold a three-day children's crusade, a fun-filled, action-packed time with the children. 500 children would constitute a small crusade, with 3000 to 4000 being present at our larger crusades. Our main aim was to lead children to a saving knowledge and relationship with Jesus. Children are so easy to lead to Christ: they don't reason and analyse, and I can truly say I have had the privilege of leading tens of thousands of children to Jesus. Occasionally the Lord would lead us to pray for the children to receive the baptism in the Holy Spirit. Many of the children would start speaking in tongues. I remember a testimony of a girl who was from the Seventh Day Adventist church, but whilst at the crusade she received the

Holy Spirit and started speaking in tongues, then prayed for her sick friend and the friend was healed! She went running home ecstatically, excited to tell her mum of the great things the Lord had done. How does a family from the Seventh Day Adventist church deal with a daughter who is filled with the Spirit and on fire for God? I don't know, but I leave these situations in God's hands!

Life in Zimbabwe during 2007 and 2008 was an interesting experience as the hyper-inflation influenced every aspect of life and society. Shops were empty, commodities difficult to access, salaries failed to cover the cost of living and sickness and death prevailed. Children suffered the most. We continued to reach out with the good news of Jesus Christ, the only hope for such hopeless situations. God favoured us with an open door to minister the Gospel in schools. Taking the most advantage of the situation, we worked tirelessly to reach as many schools as we could physically manage. One headmaster offered us the whole school for the week, as most teachers were on strike due to salaries that barely bought a loaf of bread. Declining his offer, we did take a long morning to bring the life-giving message of the Gospel to the teenagers of Zimbabwe. The Gospel is the only message of true hope that you can offer anyone in a desperate situation, and what a privilege it was to give the free gift of the Gospel to the youth of Zimbabwe.

Leading thousands of young people to Christ was somehow never enough. There were so many millions more to reach. It was in 2008 that the Lord gave me this dream of reaching more children. It came in the form of a question: "How many more children can we reach if we can reproduce a children's crusade but put it on the TV?" Initially it was like a joke! I didn't take the question too seriously but the seed began to grow in my heart. It grew into something real, a passion, a dream, a vision: to make children's programmes to reach more children with the good news of Jesus Christ. This vision grew into a confidence that this is what I must do and that God was going to make it happen.

And happen it did. 'Tommy Time' was produced, a puppet program: 13 series, 25minutes each and currently being broadcast on Zimbabwe and Zambia TV. Mwana Ministries was registered as a Scottish charity in May 2011—to oversee the work of producing children's TV programmes, running after school clubs in compounds of Lusaka, like Chiasa where it all began, and to pay school fees for orphans to go to school.

This is only the beginning, but all Glory must go to God, for taking a fear-filled Scottish girl and changing her, using her to reach the children of Africa. If God can do this with me, I am confident he can do even greater things in your life!

Janey Menzies
Mwana Ministries
www.mwanaministries.org

Editor's note: **Mwana Ministries** seeks to improve the lives of children in Africa and beyond by reaching them with the good news of Jesus Christ and by providing opportunities for furthering their education. The separate arms of Mwana Ministries are Mwana Media, Mwana Mission and Mwana Action. For anyone wishing to support or to partner with Mwana Ministries, donations can be made through the website at **www.mwanaministries.org**

MY TIME IN BORNEO

Robert Torrance

I WILL START at the beginning of my walk with God.
I am one of ten—seven brothers and three sisters. My
father was Roman Catholic whereas my mother belonged to
the Church of Scotland. My father's side had a bigger say
in how we worshipped, especially since mother's mother
had passed away. (Her father had disowned her on grounds
of religion.) Anyway, we were moved from school to
school (Protestant—Catholic) and so were unsettled in our
beliefs. When we moved to Tullibody we were enrolled in
a Protestant school and my mum and dad joined St Serf's
Church.

In the 1950's Reverend Ian Cowie came to St Serf's in
Tullibody. He was a great man who knew God. From the
way he talked about Christianity it was clear that this man
was chosen—he knew the Master. Mr Cowie would walk
round the whole village talking to all he met. The miners
who had worked their shift from 6 a.m. to 2 p.m. would
gather at the Cross (Fraser's shop). Ian would stand among
them and talk about Jesus, giving his testimony about how
he was called into the ministry. He would visit homes to
tell people the Good News, showing them that there is a
better way.

One day Mr Cowie paid us a home visit. We were all
present except for my oldest brother. He had stayed with
our grandparents while at St Ninian's, a Catholic
comprehensive school in Glasgow. He was baptised as a
Roman Catholic and had to stay with our grandparents. He

was involved in trotting horses and didn't want to leave St Ninian's.

Mr Cowie suggested we join St Serfs Church, so one Sunday morning we all went to church to be baptised— which was on 22nd March 1959. That was a speech day. We used to have woodland services where we would gather with all our friends and carry banners and head up through the village Cross, the Ham & Egg Breas (the name of an area of Tullibody where we used to meet to worship) to the Prince of Wales curling pond. One of the church leaders would lead us in singing hymns and got us all talking about Jesus, the church and what it means to be a Christian. These were encouraging times.

In 1961 I joined the Army. I enlisted into the 1st Battalion K.O.S.B. (the King's Own Scottish Borderers). I was billeted at Berwick where we did our training. We were first posted to Aden. The territory was barren hilly land where the locals lived in homes cut into the hills. There were terrorists who would snipe at us, and indeed there were a few casualties. We had to look out for landmines, booby traps, and, of course, snipers—it was a bad situation. The wadis were more dangerous as it meant we were on low ground and the so-called enemy were shooting down on us. We were certainly glad when we finished our time in Aden.

Our next posting was Borneo. We went to Hong Kong for our initial training in jungle warfare. From there we were transferred to Malaya where the real training began. We were based at the Jungle Warfare School where we were made aware of and trained to deal with the dangers we would face in Borneo.

After our training we flew to Sibu, in Borneo. From there we were moved to the base Long Jawi from where we would take up our missions. It was during the patrols that our duty began in earnest and where our training was put to the test. I was wireless operator for Charlie Company

Platoon. The helicopter would drop us off at a landing zone in the jungle, from where we would patrol. We were in constant contact with base the whole time we came under fire, and we frequently needed increasing support—and often back-up as well.

One morning I rose feeling as though I had 'flu. I felt weak and unable to move. I wasn't able to carry the radio so I asked for help. The Section Commander recognised that I was very ill and told me we would have to call in for an air lift. We managed to set up the radio and make contact with base. I was coughing up blood by this time.

When the helicopter arrived a rope ladder was dropped with a harness so that I could be winched up into the chopper. On arrival at Sibu, almost unconscious, I was helped into a Land Rover and rushed to hospital.

It was during my stay in hospital that I had an amazing experience! I found myself descending underground on some sort of vessel—it was like an underground tunnel with muddy banks on either side. Threatening malevolent creatures emerged from the mud with clenched fists and were saying, "We'll get you!" This went on for a while and the vessel I was on started going up the tunnel—and the last thing I remember about being in that tunnel has stuck in my mind ever since. I emerged into what I can only describe as a beautiful garden, full of intense colour and unbelievable peace. Then I was looking into this marvellous light—so bright and blinding that I had to shut my eyes. It was unquestionably a miraculous if not supernatural experience, yet very real!

Meanwhile the Army had got in touch with Major Tullis who got a message through to my parents to be on standby to fly out to Borneo—since my life was in the balance to the extent that there wasn't much hope for my survival. The congregation at St Serf's Church were informed, and prayers were said for me.

In spite of all odds I began to pull through and was sent to the Cameron Highland, in Malaya, to recuperate. I was soon well enough to return to Sibu and on my arrival there the medical officer wanted to consult me. I'll never forget his words on seeing me! He greeted me with a handshake and called me 'the world's miracle man'!

Something miraculous certainly did happen to me. My internal organs were in effect on shutdown—a disease they called Leptospirosis—an infection accompanied by severe fever, often fatal, as a result of dirty water, rats and leaches.

I thank and praise the Lord for giving me life!

I am so grateful for that miraculous experience, which has made me realise the power of prayer. As a result of it, too, my faith has grown from strength to strength, with the blessed assurance that our Lord, who lives in light unapproachable, is surely ever-present, even in our darkest moments.

Robert Torrance
Tullibody, Scotland

FROM DARKNESS TO LIGHT

Linda McAllister

I'LL NEVER FORGET the first time I saw Linda. I had participated in the morning service in our local Church of Scotland by reading an extract from the pre-prepared sermon the minister had printed out to be read by various volunteers in his absence. After the final hymn and prayer, followed by the long drawn-out threefold 'Amen' sung by the congregation, the various readers lined up at the church door to shake the hands of the congregation as they filed out. I had never seen her before, but Linda engaged my attention the minute she appeared before me and grasped my hand. I thought afterwards, she was like a red rose amidst the mundane black and grey outfits of the other worshippers. Also, she was effusive in her thanks, which surprised me since I'd only read one small portion of the sermon. "You're welcome," I said, "I hope you might join our little prayer group on Tuesday evenings."

She let go my hand and moved on to the next handshaker in the line. Before long everyone had passed onto the green lawn outside, but I was still aware of the musical twitter of her Scottish accent as various members of the congregation thronged around her.

She was very effusive, almost over-friendly, while others looked slightly embarrassed, some staring at her, even shaking their heads. Then it occurred to me—this brightly coloured, effusive and fluttering songbird was quite tipsy. I learnt later that she was an alcoholic and had come to the church service in an earnest attempt to turn a page and find a new source of strength in the Lord.

She duly attended the prayer meetings on Tuesdays, very effusive in her enthusiasm but clearly still under the influence of spirit rather than Spirit! She was at least a colourful and flamboyant addition to the group who valued her attendance. But then, suddenly, she stopped coming and wasn't seen again for a number of weeks.

In the days that followed I found myself driven to pray in earnest for her. I did not know then where she lived, but I walked along the streets of Tullibody as I prayed, thinking she must be close, nearby. Week after week went by and I kept up my prayerful vigil, and the prayer group regularly prayed for her on Tuesday evenings. During the weeks that went by the prayer group took it for granted that Linda was no longer coming to the group. It was all the more surprising, therefore, that when I walked into the church hall one Tuesday early in December, she was there, at her old place next to Robert, the leader of the group. She turned and smiled, a sweet soft smile, as I walked by. I fleetingly touched her fresh auburn hair and said, "So nice to see you again, Linda." I took my usual seat at the other end of the table and said, "Thank you, Lord, thank you!"

I looked at her and saw that her face had been scrubbed clean of all make-up, exposing a blotchy red surface, even marred by what looked like a rash of pimples. Apart from that, she had a worn, ravaged look. She was unusually quiet and said nothing during the discussions, and did not offer a prayer during the prayer session. What I didn't know then was that she had been 'drying out', struggling to emerge from the Slough of Despond into which she had fallen.

When I entered the church the following Sunday morning I saw that Linda was there, alone, in her usual place against the wall in a back row immediately in front of the church entrance. Clearly she was completely sober. She looked elegant in a stylish black coat and long, flowing white silk scarf.

Six months have gone by since that first Sunday when I saw her, and what a different Linda she is now—always perfectly poised and clearly a very competent woman, as one can tell by the controlled syntax and eloquence of her testimony, which I asked her to write so that it can be included in this volume. I called this collection of testimonies *Touched by Angels*—but if you have met the new sober Linda, you would know without question that you have been touched by an angel.—*Charles Muller*.

*   *   *

THIS TESTIMONY IS DEDICATED TO:

My Mother and Father

**Charles Muller, without whose help, support and co-operation
I would not have had the courage to write it**

And to Bert Rodger for his continued Love and Patience

A S I RECALL, my story began when I was around
three years old.

I was the first-born child to working class parents—Annie
Anderson Todd (my mother) and Hugh Stewart McAllister
(my father). My father was a Coal Miner for the most part
of his life, eventually being promoted to Mine Deputy at
Solsgirth Coal Mine, Dollar. My mother worked in one of
the local Mills, then ended her working career as a
Pharmacy Assistant in Marshall's Chemist, Alva. When I
was five years old I was enrolled at Dalmore Primary
School and attended Sunday School at the Baptist Church,
both in Alva. I was a very shy little girl but I remember
thoroughly enjoying my Sunday-School Classes and was
always reading my Bible. So much so, that my mother
thought I would eventually become a Minister. I was also
enrolled in ballet classes and enjoyed singing and dancing.

I am the eldest of two other sisters—Wendy who is now 50
years old and Charlotte who is 37 years old. Both my
sisters are extremely attractive, but have very different
personalities. Wendy is outgoing and likes to talk a lot.
She also has a daughter named Jennifer, my only niece.
From what I have gathered, she also enjoys talking!
Charlotte is outgoing, too, but differs from Wendy in that

she has decided, along with her husband Colin, to put most of her energy into her career; in this she has excelled and I am very proud of her. Actually, I am proud of both my sisters. I also have a daughter, Melissa, who is 26 years old. Melissa is a beautiful girl with a bubbly and outgoing personality. I don't see an awful lot of Melissa now, but mostly that was my fault. I would hardly say I was the best role model for her at that time. It is the one important thing in my life that I very much regret and if I could change it I would. If she reads this book I would want her to know that I love her, miss her and would give anything to have made her young life better.

When I was around three years old, my father had a serious accident at Dollar Coal Mine. His leg was run over by an underground rail car. Someone was supposed to press a red button to warn him the car was on its way—it came unexpectedly and the wheel cut off his leg. Afterwards the leg was amputated high up on the thigh. When the accident happened he was left bleeding and used his belt as a tourniquet to slow down the blood loss while he waited to be rescued. Ever since—he was twenty-one at the time—he has had a wooden leg. I can still remember his accident to this day and being taken by my mother to see him in hospital. At the time it happened I think I was too young to take in the full extent of his accident, but when I was older I understood the situation a lot better. I cannot imagine how my mother and father dealt with the accident, as they were not long married at the time, but somehow both of them managed to get through it together.

In the early days he was reluctant to go on the beach wearing a swimsuit. Even so, if we did go to the seaside he would sit there, on the beach, with his wooden leg and not dare to go into the water, yet long to do so. He did not want to attract attention to himself but at length we persuaded him to take off the leg and we helped him into the water. The attention he attracted was short lived and in no time he was swimming once again, revelling in it. He had always been a strong swimmer.

I spent a lot of time at my grandparents' house from the age of three and I remember that every chance I had, I just could not wait to go and spend time with both of them. They were my father's parents—Joseph and Marion McAllister. They both lived in Harthill for a number of years, eventually staying in Whitburn, East Lothian. I adored them both, especially my grandfather. He was a very quiet man, easy-going and a perfect gentleman. He died of cancer when I was 19 years old and I still remember the last day I ever saw him. He was upstairs in bed and my Aunt Joyce was sitting in the room beside him. I went straight over to him and cuddled him. When I walked towards the door of his bedroom I turned around and looked at him again. He looked back at me and waved. I knew then that we would never see each other again. I was heartbroken and took his death much harder than any of my family really knew. I think about him most days even now.

In those early days we did go for holidays, but not very often since there was not a lot of money to go around then. I remember going on holiday to Blackpool for the first time with my mother, father, sister Wendy and my grandparents. It was our first holiday there and I remember it was very cold all the time. The only part of the holiday Wendy and I enjoyed was the Pleasure Beach with its endless amounts of shows. I am glad we did not go back there again.

My favourite holiday was the two or three times we went to a beautiful little fishing village called Portmahomack near Dingwall, Scotland. It only had one Hotel—The Caledonian—and it had a farm, which was home to absolutely hundreds of Corgi pups. I would visit my friend Jane at the farm sometimes and the pups were small, cuddly and very friendly. I loved our times spent holidaying there. We would go and sit on the sandy beach for hours and my Uncle John would take us out in his Cabin Cruiser and Speedboat. It was great fun. Usually, he would drive the boats very fast and sometimes we would all get a soaking.

Oh, how I remember feeling the gentle breeze covering my whole body with the warm sunshine! During the night, I would lie awake in our Caravan just listening to the sound of the waves sweeping across the shore line.

When I was 14 years old I was enrolled at Alva Academy, in 1973. I enjoyed my days at School but, because I was tall and very thin, I was always being picked on and called names. When I left the Secondary School I gained five O-Levels—English, History, Mathematics, Geography and Food & Nutrition. I then received a place at Clackmannan College of Further Education, where I studied Secretarial Work and Accounting. I was there for two years and gained good passes upon leaving. Not long before I left the College, I was already attending the Old Parish Church in Alva, where my mother had me baptised—when I was 16 years old.

In 1976 I was offered my first position as an Office Junior with the Forth Valley Health Board in Stirling. After four years I was promoted to Shorthand Typist in the Finance Department and three years later I got my final promotion to Personal Assistant to the Area Management Accountant. During this time, I got married, in 1983, to a very nice man named Bobby Brynes, who was both quiet and hard-working. Unfortunately, the marriage did not work out and we divorced in 1992. I worked for the Health Board until

1986, when I left to have my daughter, Melissa. By that time, I had also fallen away from the Church, although I somehow never lost my faith and belief in God.

During my time with the Health Board I was introduced to a very different world to which I had been familiar with. I came from a background where I had been very protected and sheltered; not surprisingly, perhaps, I was extremely shy and inward, with the inability to make friends easily. Starting work opened many different types of opportunities for me. I began to open up to people and started socialising with my workmates. I now had money and was able to buy nice clothes, perfumes and make-up, which hitherto I never had the opportunity of having. Unfortunately, my life was to change quite dramatically. Now I had been introduced to the world of Alcohol.

My job was held open for me, but I decided to leave my post and take time out to look after Melissa. When Melissa reached Primary School age, I went back to work as a Personal Assistant to Mr John Nicol, Minister, Holy Trinity Church in Bridge-of-Allan. I thoroughly enjoyed my time working with him and was sad to leave after three years. I then signed up with the Stirling Employment Agency as a Temporary Personal Assistant, where I enjoyed numerous high-profile assignments. This included working with the Academic Registrar of Stirling University, the Director of the Scottish Police College and Professor Ron Roberts, Managing Director of Landcatch Natural Selection. The latter position dealt with the anatomy of Salmon. It was at this point in my life that alcohol, without me actually realising it, was beginning to take a hold on me and my drinking was increasing. Instead of it only being on a Friday or Saturday night, it was now taking place on some week-nights and bar lunches were increasing as well. I had been blaming my drinking on my ex-husband, my mother and father, the rest of my family, the workplace, bosses, but did not stop to realise that it was actually my own fault— that I was the reason for my drinking. I was still able to hold a job at this time, but it was becoming increasingly difficult for me to focus properly on my family and my work. I was physically becoming more ill, sometimes taking dizzy spells at work and having to go home early. Eventually, I was relieved of my position at work because of alcohol abuse. I simply was now becoming unable and unreliable to hold down a job. I could not even trust myself. As well as all this, I had started to experience black-outs, sometimes not even remembering what I had done the night before. A couple of times I had to be sent to Stirling Royal Infirmary and detained overnight because of delirium tremors (D.T's). During all of this mayhem, I am, however, glad that I never was violent due to my alcoholism.

I know now that nothing or nobody was to blame for my misuse of alcohol, because at the beginning I only used it as a crutch believing my problems would simply vanish—how wrong was I.

Looking back at my life, and if I'm being completely honest, my real problems started with men. I was a virgin until the age of 18 and lost it to my mother's cousin. I was completely unaware that he was related to my mother and did not find out about this until, one night, my father returned home from the Pub and confronted me. I was astonished and felt thoroughly ashamed of myself, but, instead of lying to him, I confessed the truth. He told me I was never to see this man again and he never spoke to me for at least three months. I guess my mother felt a little bit sorry for me for she never mentioned it to me.

Well, it wasn't a very promising baptism into the world of men, was it? After this happened I was left feeling totally unsure of myself and not very trusting of men in general.

It was a long time before I had another boyfriend and during the experience just mentioned I had stopped eating. I am not sure why, but I became very ill and lost an awful lot of weight. I was already a fairly thin person anyway, but the extreme loss of weight became dangerously low. Both my parents were very distressed and called our doctor in to assess me. Straightaway he advised me and my parents that I had Anorexia Nervosa. When I heard this I was shocked though I am not sure why. The doctor wrote me a prescription for a bottle of vitamin tonic and about two to three weeks later, I started to gain an appetite and was eating regularly again.

Unfortunately, my relationships with men, including my ex-husband and ex-partner, did not go as I hoped they would. I guess alcohol played the biggest part in the eventual downfall of those relationships. Deep down all I really wanted was a loving relationship with a man, both mentally and physically. Unfortunately, I achieved neither. I have never given up hope that maybe, someday, someone will enter into my life that can give me both of these things. Let's face it, I have a lot of love left to give.

When I was separated from my husband, Melissa and I went to live with my parents at their house in Alva. I had not long come out of hospital after suffering a breakdown, and my parents felt I would be more comfortable with them. My time with them was particularly trying as I did not realise I had become so used to running my own home and being my own boss. Melissa, on the other hand, was suffering badly through the break-up as well and she was behaving very badly. She kept asking me when we were going back to live with Daddy. I felt heartbroken and was at a loss to tell her the truth. We would not be going back. I was completely guilt ridden and it took me a long time to forgive myself for hurting her in such a way.

After about three months, I got myself a part-time position as a Sales Assistant with Taylor and Roche, TV and Aerial Engineers in Alloa. It was during my time working there that I met my partner Alex. He was a mature student at Heriot Watt University in Edinburgh, where he graduated with a first class degree in chemistry. Alex only worked at the shop on Saturdays. He seemed to get on well and after a while we became friends. When I look back at this relationship, I now realise that I only thought I loved him and when he eventually asked me to rent a private house with him, I said yes. My parents spoke to me about this and advised me that they thought it was too soon for me to move in with Alex and that he had caught me on the re-bound. It was not until we moved in together that I realised we did not really have an awful lot in common. He was a nice person, but started to become possessive and domineering towards me. In other-words, my parents had been right

Alex got on well with Melissa at the beginning, but eventually they started arguing with each other. She would do something he did not like and he would get on at her. She would then always turn round and inform him that, as he was not her father, he could not tell her what to do. It was like being in the middle of a war zone. During this time, I had a dog named Shep. I reared him from a pup and he lived until he was around 13 years old. I am so glad for the gift of Shep, because he remained a true and loyal friend to me and I would have been so lonely without him. However, when Shep died, things just got worse and Alex and I ended up like ships passing in the night. We hardly spoke to each other and the silences in the house were eerie. Melissa had gone to stay with her father for a while as he had asked me if it would be alright for him to get to know her a little better. Melissa's father had married again, but unfortunately Melissa did not get on with his new wife and sadly made her life extremely difficult. Eventually, Melissa had no choice but to come back and live with me and Alex. As usual, I found solace in the bottom of a bottle and I left Alex.

It is hard to believe, that for the past 30 years or so, the only objective of my desire came in the form of a wine bottle. This is the way that alcohol affects your body and mind when it is being abused. Your whole way of thinking and reasoning becomes totally distorted and your physical being becomes weak. I was always a quiet person, but towards the end of my alcoholic years, I simply became very withdrawn and tended to stay indoors. I was not looking after myself. I had stopped wearing nice clothes and make-up and just did not care how I looked any more or what people thought of me. Nothing seemed to be of any importance to me anymore. I am positive that the consumption of lots of alcohol gave me the confidence to talk to people, especially men.

In 1997, when I was still with my partner Alex, I decided to go along to my first meeting of Alcoholics Anonymous. I thought I would be nervous, but surprisingly I was calm and looking forward to it. Everybody was seated around a circular table with the Chairperson and the person who was talking about their experience, strength and hope at the top. I remember everyone came and shook my hand and asked me what my first name was. They were very nice people and made me feel very welcome.

The speaker told us about his life with alcohol for about three quarters of an hour, and then we stopped to have tea, coffee and biscuits. After about 15 minutes we all took our seats again and this time the chairperson asked each person in the room if they would like to say anything or maybe want to talk about something that was bothering us. I said nothing. However, I did enjoy my first meeting and met one or two really nice people. I continued to go to the meetings in Tullibody every Wednesday morning and Friday night. Eventually, when I became the Secretary of the Group, I would make up sandwiches and rolls for them every Friday night. There was one particular man there who I knew had been sleeping rough for a while and he was so small and thin. I guess I took pity on him and every Friday night, if there were any sandwiches/rolls left over, I would wrap them up for him so that he at least would have something to eat.

I managed to get nine months sobriety under my belt until I started receiving some unwanted attention from a man who ran the group and had actually founded it some 33 years ago. Although I had been sober for some time now, I was still a bit vulnerable and not back to my full physical strength. I have heard it can take a long time for an alcoholic to fully recover. However, this man singled me out for special attention. He knew I was vulnerable at the time and absolutely took advantage of this. You know, I am not usually a person who is easily taken in by someone, but I honestly thought he was only trying to make me feel comfortable and a real part of the group. His house was in the newest part of Tullibody and he always gave me a lift home. For a long time his behaviour seemed normal enough and he would talk about things to do with AA and usually what he was involved in. I remember him telling me that he travelled to Southern Ireland and Spain quite often, to take part in AA Conferences where usually he would be asked to speak. He was well known in different parts of the world due to his extensive knowledge of alcohol abuse. However, if only I had known then what I know now. It transpires that this person had been well known for picking on newer and younger members of AA, particularly females. He would give them a lift home and then suggest that they stop at a nearby pub for a drink. Once he had managed to help them get drunk, he would then take advantage of them. For a man of his long experience in AA this sort of behaviour was totally unacceptable and quite unbelievable. I suppose you could say he enjoyed collecting trophies. He had started to become far too familiar with me and at one point suggested that it would do me the world of good if I were to have liaisons sexually with him and his partner. That was it! I was disgusted with him and told him I would certainly not take part in sexual activities of that nature. I remember him laughing at me uproariously when I said this and he told me it was high time I relaxed a little and got a life. I am not sure what happened to me after this, but I know I became anxious when the meetings came round and I think I had become a little afraid of him. I started going to different meetings, but everywhere I went he always turned up and I just felt as if I could not get away from him. Eventually, I felt threatened to the point that it might have been perceived he was stalking me. The problem was, I could not actually take action against him for anything; after all, he had not physically tried to hurt me. However, I knew it could have been construed as mental cruelty.

Anyhow, not long after all this, I turned to the only thing I thought would give me comfort and save me—you've guessed it—the bottle. Oh, what a mess! After having done so well and looking and feeling so much better I went and ruined it all by taking that first drink. I cannot blame this man for me drinking again, but from then on I had nothing more to do with him. As far as I am concerned he is what people would class as a sexual predator and he is well known for this type of behaviour throughout AA. The thing that hurt the most was the fact that the AA members who had known me for a long time did not have the courage and sense of responsibility to take me aside and warn me about this. If only I had known this, things would have been very different. Anyway, I suppose that's life. Sometimes it can hit you with some pretty powerful stuff, as long as you learn from these experiences, or at least become more aware of situations like that. So, that was the end of my time in AA – I never went back but have never forgotten the genuine people I met there and think about them from time to time.

In the midst of this confusion, I was still feeling physically unwell and was advised to have a total hysterectomy by my doctor. I was beginning to lose more blood than I should have when my monthly cycle came around. I was still quite young at the time, probably 40 years old. However, I thought about this long and hard and decided to go through with the operation. I stayed in hospital for three weeks and took around four months to recover.

However, some months after I recovered I started drinking yet again. If I thought my life was bad, it was to become horrendous. I had no friends and my family had simply had enough and washed their hands of me. I was not living life, but just existing. My life was now about to reach rock bottom and at the time I just did not give a damn. Nothing in the world mattered. A stupid thought ran across my mind that I could end it all, but then I realised I probably would not make a good job of that either. I had started to go out at nights to the pub again and with no fear in the world, I would simply find myself in situations that, had I been sober, would never have ended up in. As a drunk woman, I was allowing myself to be taken advantage of and had not realised how dangerous life was becoming. In the meantime, my mother had become a member of Al-Anon, a group that gives support to the family and friends of alcoholics. Somehow or other, she began to learn more about alcoholism and we started to get on better with each other than we ever had. I know she was now beginning to understand my situation much better. After that, other family members seemed to have more time for me and also became more understanding.

Thank God for this, somewhere out there a flicker of hope was wavering for me. My life was not over, at least, not yet. I knew that deep down there was a new Linda about to emerge—a much stronger and confident one than I could have possibly imagined. More importantly, a sober one.

A few months after I left Alex, I bumped into a man I had not seen for some years, in the Tullibody Inn. His name is Bert Rodger and we sat and talked and drank for the rest of the afternoon. By the end of that day both of us were rather drunk and he invited me back to his house. I remember him telling me he had known my parents for a long time and that his wife Jean had died a few years back.

After a while of getting to know him a bit better, he asked me if I would like to come and live in his home. I had to think about it carefully, but decided it might be alright. Bert was living in the house rent free as his sister owned it and we both agreed that I could have a roof over my head as long as I kept the house tidy, did the cooking and the washing and ironing. At first, we did not really get along. Bert is a very kind and gentle man, who in general does not keep well and has been known to lose his temper quite quickly. I found it difficult to get used to this but eventually managed to get my way around him. I am still with Bert

and do the best I can to look after him and make sure he
eats his meals. We also have a dog named Buster, who is a
pure bred Staffordshire Bull Terrier. Buster is a big, gentle
giant of a dog and I absolutely love him to bits. Our house
just would not be the same without Buster in it. He has
arthritis in one of his back legs due to his age, but he still
loves to get out in the mornings for a walk. I know that
both Bert and Buster need me and that I am just so glad that
I am sober and able to do this for them.

About five months ago I had my last drunk episode. I had
now reached absolute rock bottom and I knew deep in my
heart that I did not have much longer to live. I had the
worst DTs I have ever experienced. I was not only seeing
and hearing things that were not real, but mentally and
physically I just could not take any more. I had never felt
so lost and lonely and kept thinking to myself, why had I
ruined the last 35 years or so? Now, I felt there was
nothing more to keep living for and that nobody really
cared.

Bert was lost. I knew he was really concerned about me,
but never showed it. He decided to take matters in to his
own hands and phoned for my doctor to visit me at home. I
argued with him at first, telling him I would be okay. But
Bert knew by the pitiful state of me that I had no choice but
to let him have his way. My doctor came out and advised
me that maybe it would be better if he had me admitted to
hospital. I dreaded the thought of this and eventually, after
a long talk with him, he let me have my way. There was
one condition, that I agreed to take a reducing prescription
of Chlordiazepoxide (Librium). This is a drug that you
absolutely cannot take alcohol with—to do so would result
in a heart attack.

After the doctor left, I was sitting on the floor, alone in my bedroom. I am not sure how long I sat there, but it seemed a while. I remember thinking how glad I was that Bert had actually called for my doctor. I knew how ill I had become.

Now I have come to the most important and life-changing part of my story.

From my bedroom window you can see clearly St Serf's Church Steeple. I stood there just staring at it and remembered asking God—please help me. I thought I could cure my alcoholism on my own, but now I really needed his help and knew I could not be saved from the black hole I was in without him. I asked him to take hold of my hand and pull me up. He answered my prayers and did just that! It was a strange yet wonderful feeling and somehow I stopped shaking and felt an inner calmness. After five years my bedroom seemed very quiet and I then became aware of a feeling of being at peace with a new sense of tranquillity. It is very difficult to explain to another human being what happened next.

After a few days of sobering up and feeling slightly more human, I suddenly announced to Bert that I was getting myself washed and dressed and going to the church. He looked at me in utter disbelief and started to laugh. In all honesty though, just after the above took place, I did fall off the wagon and had gone to the church rather intoxicated. I do remember walking through the doors of the church and feeling that I did belong there. I do not have a clue what the members of the kirk must have thought of me. They were, in general, very nice and slightly amused at the sight of this overly painted drunk woman.

There is another reason why I am so glad I joined the Church. I met a gentleman called Charles and I have to say

I could never have met a more sincere or kind person. I did not know it then, but he was to become one of the most important parts of my life. At last, I had found what I had been searching for all these years—my soul mate and best friend.

I realised that God had given me a second chance at having a new and much better life than before. The old, inebriated Linda had now turned into a new person and a born-again Christian. Although throughout my life I have always had faith in God, I felt my faith was now much stronger than before and, as each day passed, I was becoming more confident and positive. I am now looking forward to the future and have the strength to deal with whatever life flings at me. I am no longer frightened of the dark or of dying.

On reflection, I have a lot of things I would still like to accomplish in my life and a lot of love to give to whoever needs it. My life up to now has been filled with both good and bad times. Unfortunately, the bad times have far outweighed the good. I have asked myself often, "Is there anything that I would change in my past?" The answer is no. I think God has been testing me all of my life and he only gives me assignments that he knows I can handle. He has been quietly guiding me throughout my life and still is. I feel his presence with me always and, strangely enough, know that I am one of his precious lambs and he will never turn his back on me.

Before I go to sleep at night, I always say my prayers and read passages out of my Bible. When I read different parts of the Bible, I feel as if I already know what has been written. It's as if I had actually lived at that time. What an uncanny feeling to have. I keep a book at my bedside called *God Calling* which tells you about the power of love and joy that restores faith and serenity in our troubled world. This book is an inspiration to me and helps give me the strength to carry on a day at a time.

Finally, I would like to end with the following passage written by Reinhold Niebuhr. It is one of my favourites and quite simply says it all:-

Living one day at a time,

Enjoying one moment at a time.

Accepting hardship as a pathway to peace.

Taking this world as it is,

Not as I would have it.

Trusting that you

Will make all things right

If I surrender to your will.

So that I may be reasonably happy in this life

And supremely happy with you in the next.

AMEN

Linda McAllister
Tullibody, Scotland

AFTERWORD

If anyone reading this book has had similar experiences of God's miraculous power or love, I would like to hear from you. Perhaps you have had a miraculous healing, an encounter with angels, or have had a near-death experience where you were transformed by the loving energy of God. Or perhaps you know of someone who has had such experiences that amount to extra-biblical proof of God's power and of a life beyond the grave.

If so, send me your testimonies, or encourage others to send theirs, for I may be able to use them in a follow-up to this inspirational book, thereby helping, comforting, strengthening and encouraging others. Send the testimonies to Charles Muller at the following address:

Diadem Books, 16 Lethen View, Tullibody, ALLOA, FK10 2GE, Scotland United Kingdom.

Email: charles@diadembooks.com

Web site: www.diadembooks.com

Other Christian books written or edited by Charles Muller

The Christian Teachings of Charles Kingsley
by Charles Muller

Diadem Books, 2011 ISBN 978-1908026033

The moral purpose of Charles Kingsley's novels is pronounced because he was a preacher, and more specifically, a teacher. He was above all a preacher of stirring didactic sermons. It is the didactic content of his writings-in his sermons, his novels, and his essays on natural theology-which is the study of this work. One too often forgets that Kingsley was not, in the first instance, a social and political reformer. As a preacher, and as a writer, he was pre-eminently a teacher-a theologian, yes, but more importantly, a Christian didactician. He was not an evangelical preacher, yet the Christian gospel was at the heart of his teachings and his moral exhortations. This work attempts to look at the Christian message that was the inspiration behind his socio-religious gospel. Writing at the time of Charles Darwin, Kingsley saw no reason to lose his sound Christian faith with the emergence of Darwin's theory of evolution. Instead, he could accept it as a means to a divine end, another example of how Providence might bring about the Kingdom of God on earth.

Touched by God
Testimonies of Christian Power

Seven inspirational testimonies edited by Charles Muller
Writers Club Press   ISBN 0-595-09413-9

Touched by God brings together seven inspirational stories
of God's supernatural intervention in the lives of Christian
believers. They constitute extra-biblical proof of God's
divine power and love.

More information at www.diadembooks.com/Touched.htm

Review of *Touched by God*:

God can Touch you too! Just trust Him. April 1, 2002
Reviewer: Emelia Hardy from Dover, N.H. United States.

The author Charles Muller will take you through the stories
of seven different people—one of them being himself. Each
story will grab you in a different way. Each will touch your
heart and soul. Some are very sad, but the author shows the
reader how brave these people are, how much they trusted
in the Lord day by day. He tells of a young boy who was
wise beyond his years and how his wisdom lay in his love
for God. This little boy's faith alone was an inspiration to
me. The story that Charles Muller tells of himself took my
breath away. His words alone made me feel his pain, his
emptiness, his longing for a God that he thought was no
longer there! He tells of a story that happened at four in the
morning that brought him to say, "God, I Love You!" This
little book, *Touched by God*, is a must read. It gave me an
inward peace that is hard to explain. It was almost as
though God touched me as I read it!

Have Anything You Really Really Want: A Christian Testimony
by Charles Muller

An inspirational guide to achieving one's goals and dreams of success.
Writers Club Press ISBN 0-595-091-539

More information at www.diadembooks.com/Youcan.htm

Have Anything You Really Really Want! is a thought-provoking study about the power of positive thinking and the Christian faith. It follows the author's own personal journey of faith and discovery as he details how his Christian faith unleashed a positive power—in the attainment of personal, even material goals (including the acquisition of university degrees and a Rolls Royce!), but more significantly in the realisation of far-reaching goals: the discovery of his wife and ultimately the transition from university professor in South Africa to successful hotel-owner in Scotland.

An important lesson in the experience of mid-life change is seen in the close dependence on God's love and boundless supply for all needs, material and spiritual.

From establishing an objective, working out a strategy, and using faith and initiative, this detailed thesis explores the essential principles for personal success and achievement and guides the reader step-by-step through the practical process of attaining his or her goals.

In the final analysis, however, the author asks whether it is the individual, or the invisible hand of Providence, which engineers the success—even to the extent of changing one's original goals, and changing oneself in the process.

The Cage and the Cross

A Christian novel by Charles Muller.
Writers Club Press. ISBN: 0-595-09806-1

A Christian novel of salvation based on an actual person, a prisoner in Pretoria Central Prison who committed suicide in 1975. The protagonist couldn't help falling in love, against his will. Those who knew him better tried to stop him, to draw him back, to tell him it was wrong, against the Law of God. But they couldn't stop him--because the affair was with God. Or was it? Perhaps the whole affair was just part of his imagination.

More information at www.diadembooks.com/Cage.htm

Rapture at Sea

A Christian novel by Carolyn & Humphrey Muller
Writers Club Press. ISBN 0-595-13825-X

As the year 2000 approaches for many the prospect of Christ's promised return becomes more of a reality. So what if the Parousia, or the Rapture *does* take place? What if Christ returns to Earth while some are at sea? Would some be taken, and some left? What might happen to those passengers on a sea voyage?

More information at www.diadembooks.com/Rapture.htm

True Life Reflections: A compilation of short essays and poems
by Inez Randolph

Format: Paperback
ISBN: 0-595-33217-X
Published: Oct-2004

The real value of this inspiring little book of essays and poems is the reassurance it gives that we are not alone in our journey through life. The sincere, practical wisdom, some of which, homespun in the hard experience of life in Ghana, comes from her "Two Graces", her grandmother and mother, will uplift and encourage the reader.

More information at www.diadembooks.com/randolph.htm

The Call that Changed my Life
by Robert Peprah-Gyamfi

Format: Paperback
ISBN: 0-595-32298-0
Published: Jun-2004

This inspiring story tells of the courage of a young Ghanaian boy who, having failed to achieve his aim to become a medical doctor by attending a university in Ghana or by virtue of a scholarship to the USSR, raised funds by working on a building site in Nigeria to pay for a daring one-way flight to East Berlin to become an asylum seeker in West Berlin—a route by which he realised his dreams and became a medical doctor in Germany. It is a wonderful testimony of Christian faith.

More information at www.diadembooks.com/robert.htm

What the Bible Says is in Your Hand!
by Rev Arthur S Dunn

Format: Paperback
ISBN: 0-595-30600-4
Published: Dec-2003

A thoroughgoing research into the Bible, from creation to salvation, this book tells it like it is. No reader will be able to ignore the power of the Holy Spirit that moves the author, originally from Jamaica, or resist the simplicity of the salvation message.

More information at www.diadembooks.com/bible.htm

Stop Holding Yourself Back!
by James Symonds

Format: Paperback
ISBN: 0-595-24062-3
Publication Date: Aug-2002

When you read this book you will feel a positive power of change beginning to unleash itself within your mind and soul. Praise the Lord!

More information at www.diadembooks.com/symonds.htm

About the Editor

Photo by John Moore

Charles Humphrey Muller, MA (Wales), PhD (London), D.Ed (SA), D.Litt (UOFS), was Professor and Head of the Department of English at the University of the North (now University of Limpopo) in South Africa for ten years, and Senior Lecturer in English at the University of South Africa before that. He is the author of numerous academic textbooks and literary studies published by Oxford University Press, McGraw-Hill and Macmillan, and was editor of *Unisa English Studies* and *Communiqué*, literary journals of the University of South Africa and the University of the North. In 1988 he left his academic career to move to Scotland where he bought a small hotel—the

Kenmore Bank Hotel in Jedburgh, fifty miles south of Edinburgh—which he and his wife Joanne ran for eleven years. During this time he founded his editing and publishing business, Diadem Books. While in Scotland he wrote a number of novels, including *Rapture at Sea*, a novel written with his wife (under the pen-name 'Carolyn Charles') based on the return of Christ. He wrote the inspirational work *Have Anything You Really Really Want*, and served as editor for his wife's 'self-help' book *So You Want to Buy a Small Hotel!* After selling his hotel in Jedburgh in 2001, he and his wife have lived in the Great Glen of Scotland, Clashnessie in Sutherland, in Nova Scotia (Canada), in New Zealand, the Kingdom of Fife and currently live in Clackmannanshire in Central Scotland.

The inspirational testimonies in this volume to God's practical power were collected from people Charles Muller met and admired while still living in South Africa. The volume includes his own testimony of God's amazing power and presence—an experience which changed his life in 1984 and precipitated the move to Scotland. This testimony ('Tapping into the Spirit') has been reprinted from Charles Muller's inspirational work *Have Anything You Really Really Want*.

CPSIA information can be obtained at www.ICGtesting.com
Printed in the USA
LVOW08s0044041115

461040LV00004B/122/P